T0072392

Praise for
God of All Creation

"I love that James did this book!"

—Beth Moore

"Who helps teach James Robison about the things of God? A theologian? A fellow Baptist preacher? A famous radio host? An important senator or governor? Would you believe it's a small miniature dachshund? In *God of All Creation,* James delightfully shares the profound truths his little Princess has shown him about life, love, and living with our Master."

—Ruth Graham, author of *In Every Pew Sits a Broken Heart* and *Fear Not Tomorrow, God Is Already There*

"Scripture declares that nature offers us a glimpse into God's power and personality. In *God of All Creation,* James Robison beautifully unveils what the creatures around you communicate about you and your Creator. Get ready for a wild adventure!"

—Lisa Bevere, speaker for Messenger International and author of *Lioness Arising*

"The lessons that James draws from the antics of his beloved mini-dach, Princess, are predictably heartwarming but unpredictably insightful. As a past owner myself of a pair of these preposterously shaped creatures (Harley Davidson and Maximus Decimus), I resonate with the truths James mines from their endearing behavior and the Word of God and am greatly encouraged. I think you will be too."

— DR. E. ANDREW McQUITTY, senior pastor of Irving Bible Church, Irving, Texas

"James loves Jesus. James loves people. And now we have learned that James loves animals. This is a delightful, fun-loving, and, yes, touching read that will appeal to cold and warm noses alike!"

— KATHY TROCCOLI, recording artist, author, and speaker

God *of* All Creation

James Robison

with James Randall Robison

Life Lessons
from Pets *and* Wildlife

God *of* All Creation

WaterBrook
PRESS

GOD OF ALL CREATION
PUBLISHED BY WATERBROOK PRESS
12265 Oracle Boulevard, Suite 200
Colorado Springs, Colorado 80921

Trade Paperback 978-0-7352-8972-7
Hardcover ISBN 978-1-4000-7459-4
eBook ISBN 978-0-307-45920-6

Copyright © 2012 by James Robison
Illustrations © 2012 by Deb Hoeffner

Cover design by Mark D. Ford; cover illustration by Deb Hoeffner; author photo by
David Edmonson

Published in the United States by WaterBrook Multnomah, an imprint of the Crown
Publishing Group, a division of Penguin Random House LLC, New York.

WATERBROOK and its deer colophon are registered trademarks of Penguin Random
House LLC.

Library of Congress Cataloging-in-Publication Data
Robison, James, 1943-
   God of all creation : life lessons from pets and wildlife / James Robison with James
Randall Robison. — 1st ed.
      p. cm.
   Includes bibliographical references (p.   ).
   ISBN 978-1-4000-7459-4 — ISBN 978-0-307-45920-6 (electronic)
   1. Animals—Religious aspects—Christianity. I. Robison, James Randall. II. Title.
   BT746.R635 2012
   231.7—dc23

                              2012007305

                              146712470

With thanks to God for another
special expression of His love.
What an awesome Father who gives
His children wildlife to observe
and the special gift of pets
that love us unconditionally.
As we love His creation, they teach us
important lessons in life.

Contents

Contents

Introduction

------⟡⟡⟡------

I never dreamed a miniature dachshund could make such a profound impact on my wife, Betty, and me.

I was the first to see the six-week-old puppies at a local feed store. There they were—four black dachshund puppies and a very different, blue heeler–colored one with blue eyes. This puppy was very unusual. Of course, they were all irresistibly cute, crawling, rolling, and nipping at one another. I picked up one and looked at its little pug nose that would grow to be long, pointed, and regal. I couldn't wait to ask Betty if she would like to get one.

Her response did not surprise me, yet I was disappointed. "I don't want a dog in the house," she said. "And we travel too much. We don't have time to train it. It's too much trouble."

She was right, but I wouldn't relent. "I would love to have a lap dog to love on," I said. She still resisted, so I knew I would have to come up with a plan.

A few days later four of our grandchildren were visiting,

and I asked if they would like to go see the puppies just up the road. "Let's go! Let's go! Come on, Mimi," they cried out to Betty. She was outnumbered, so we drove to the feed store. When the grandchildren saw the puppies, you can imagine the response.

"Mimi and Papaw, let's get one! They are so cute!"

When the kids picked up several puppies and passed them around, I knew I had her. How could she resist? As Betty held them, especially the smaller, calmer one with brown eyes, she was smitten. She cupped the tiny puppy in her hands, looked into her face, and fell in love.

"Are you sure that's the one you want?" I asked. "She seems tiny and less active."

"This is the one," she replied. "This is our princess."

The grandchildren jumped for joy, especially seven-year-old Laney. We paid for the puppy, got in the car, and began a life-enriching journey. I had no idea the joy, laughter, tears, and lessons we were about to learn from that short-legged, stretched-out, slick-as-a-seal black dog with brown trim.

Princess often sits on my chest with her paws folded and her nose close to mine. I look at her and tell her how God made her so beautiful and painted her so pretty. Her distinct markings are amazing.

You are about to read some poignant lessons we can learn from pets and all creatures—a clear revelation of the love God has for each of us. I share what I've learned as I've watched, held, and loved our little Princess and as I've watched wild animals in nature. Only a God who truly loves us as individuals could bless us with such treasured moments with our pets and wildlife, if we will just take notice.

Jesus, the greatest person who ever lived, said, "Look at the birds" (Matthew 6:26), and Solomon, the wisest man, said,

"Take a lesson from the ants" (Proverbs 6:6). Both our Savior and the man renowned for his wisdom understood the deeper truths that God reveals through His creation—from foolish sheep to dangerous predators, soaring eagles, birds of prey, and even hard-working insects.

A friend once said, "If you can't see God in everything, you won't see God in anything." In this book we will explore expressions of God's love, lessons in His grace, warnings about sin, and other eternal truths as we consider our pets and other awesome residents of God's vast creation.

1

❖

The Master's Voice

Princess loves Betty and me—her "Mimi and Papaw." (Since all eleven of our grandchildren call us Mimi and Papaw, I assume Princess must think these are our names.) But her natural instincts compel her to run away at times. If I open the front door of our house and she smells a squirrel, she's off. Her intense focus to fulfill her desires could get her into serious trouble. She could run into traffic and get sideswiped by a car. She could catch her prey and find that it's not a squirrel but something more vicious and powerful. Or she could simply pursue her quarry to the point where she no longer knows how to get back home.

Oftentimes, only my voice keeps Princess from getting into trouble. If she listens and obeys, she will come back to the safety and provision of her home. If not, all manner of trouble awaits.

The prophet Isaiah pointed out, "All of us, like sheep, have strayed away. We have left God's paths to follow our own" (53:6). In his time the people understood the analogy of sheep. Shepherds were very important. Not only did they fend off predators, but they also led their sheep to green pastures for food and to clean water for drink. The "smart" sheep (relatively speaking) learned to listen to their shepherd for their own good, but even these wiser ones had a tendency to wander.

The same is true with people. Really, the question is not whether we will stray. We will, because it is in our nature to do so. The question is, what will we do when God calls us back into His care? And, even more important, will we know God's voice when He does call?

I can promise you that if Princess took off, pursuing something she shouldn't, and *you* called her, she would not respond but would keep going. She does not know you and would not recognize your voice. I suppose there is a small chance she might pause, look in your direction, and wonder, *Who is that?* But then in a flash, she would continue her chase.

You might think that if your voice is similar to mine—

deep and booming—then you might get her attention and convince her to follow your instructions. Not so! Princess knows my voice. She does not know yours.

Jesus, in identifying Himself as one with God, also related to the shepherds of His time:

> My sheep listen to my voice; I know them, and they
> follow me. I give them eternal life, and they will never
> perish. No one can snatch them away from me, for my
> Father has given them to me, and he is more powerful
> than anyone else. No one can snatch them from the
> Father's hand. The Father and I are one. (John
> 10:27–30)

Like the shepherds' sheep, pets learn their masters' voices. We, too, can learn to hear the voice of the Master. The first step is to enter His fold. This is salvation. We become a new creation and, in the process, get "new ears." Our spiritual rebirth enables us to hear things we did not hear before. Like a newborn baby, we are attuned to new sounds. But like a newborn, we cannot always discern the noises. We must mature and learn and develop a keen sense of hearing.

Jesus discussed this when He said,

> To those who listen to my teaching, more understanding will be given, and they will have an abundance of knowledge. But for those who are not listening, even what little understanding they have will be taken away from them. (Matthew 13:12)

We learn to hear His voice by listening to His teachings, found in Scripture, and by understanding them. Just as Princess's familiarity allows her to discern my voice, our familiarity with our spiritual Shepherd allows us to discern His voice. If we choose to ignore His voice, we become dull of hearing. When we choose to listen and act on His words, we are blessed, because we hear.

Clearly it is possible to discern the voice of God in our lives. If pet dogs can hear our voices, we can hear the voice of our Father in heaven! When we know and respond to His voice, He promises to lead us down the path of life. When we stray, He will call us back to His security and care. Nobody can take us away from His protection and presence if only we will learn to hear and heed the Master's voice.

2

God Will Chase Us

I enjoy taking Princess outside. She scurries about, sniffs the ground for other creatures, and follows the scent of animals long gone. Her tail is a blur of nonstop motion because she is so happy. Sometimes her excitement overcomes her, and I have to pick up my pace, or I'll lose sight of her.

One day as I was hurrying after her, I remembered Jesus's parable of the lost sheep.

If a man has a hundred sheep and one of them wanders away, what will he do? Won't he leave the ninety-nine others on the hills and go out to search for the one that is lost? And if he finds it, I tell you the truth, he will rejoice over it more than over the ninety-nine that didn't

wander away! In the same way, it is not my heavenly
Father's will that even one of these little ones should
perish. (Matthew 18:12–14)

God would rather that we stay in the safety and security of
the fold. When He leaves us "on the hills," we are not being
abandoned but rather kept in a place of provision and blessing.
But the Lord cares so deeply for those outside of His care that
He rejoices over the one who returns. In fact, the entire Bible is
the story of a good and holy God pursuing an unfaithful and
wandering people. He does not want a single one of us to perish
or live in defeat. And though that in itself is a glorious story of
devotion and love, there's much more to the relationship He
seeks with us.

As I chased Princess that day, I thought, *I don't mind
chasing you, but I don't want to do it all the time. I'd much rather
hold you.*

I find great joy simply in holding Princess. Every night
Betty puts Princess in her "taxi," which is a wicker basket with
a door that serves as a kennel. The basket sits right next to our
bed, so in the morning Betty opens the door, and Princess
emerges from beneath her blanket, stretches her long body, and
sprints to the family room. I hear her little feet pattering across

the floor until she reaches my recliner, leaps into my lap, lies down on my chest with her long nose at my chin, gives me a slobbery kiss, and looks straight up into my eyes. Then she just lies there, right next to my heart, staring into my face. She's happy and content for me to hold her, and it brings me great joy too.

Every day when I awaken, I want to run as fast as Princess does to jump into God's lap, look into His eyes, and stay close to His heart. This brings our heavenly Father great pleasure and gives me indescribable comfort, peace, and security.

As Princess lies with her paws resting on my chest, her long ears perk up, and she waits for me to speak to her. I know she can't understand my words, but I believe she senses the love I have for her. I do know that when I speak these loving words, she listens. I also know that when we learn to hear the Lord, He will speak words of encouragement and affection to us.

In a world where people seek affirmation and acceptance from so many wrong places, there is one place where they can find true appreciation and fulfillment. And while God will chase us when we go astray, real joy is found when we learn to rest in His presence.

If we will draw close to Him and perk up our ears, He will comfort and guide us.

3

⊰⊱⊰⊱

Created for a Purpose

Dachshunds are natural hunters, so when Princess was a puppy, I understood her desire to pursue what she viewed as her prey, even though she was too small to catch anything. As she matured, she became stronger and faster. I soon realized that if she started catching what she was chasing, we could have some serious problems.

First, there were armadillos. They are kind of cute in their reptilian way, and on the surface they seem completely harmless. Though they can move surprisingly fast, they are no match for a dog. Princess could catch an armadillo, and in a fight I have no doubt that she would win. Dachshunds were originally trained to chase badgers, which although small, are as fierce as grizzly bears. These little dogs can work their narrow, sleek bodies into a badger hole and use their long snouts and sharp teeth to grip their prey by the nose, which renders them helpless. The dachshund's short, stocky legs give it tremendous leverage to drag the animal out of the hole.

But I don't want Princess to chase badgers, because she could get badly hurt. Even an armadillo will scratch and bite fiercely when forced to fight for its life. We might celebrate Princess's victory in battle, but would it really be worth it if she was scratched blind or infected with rabies?

With white-tailed deer there is even more danger. Princess couldn't bring one down, but if she got too close, a deer's powerful kick to the head could kill her. So I've had to train her by saying repeatedly, "You're not a deer dog. Don't chase the deer. Leave them alone." Now she sits calmly beside me while we're watching deer. She knows they are off-limits.

I do let Princess chase rabbits because I know they are too fast for her. She loves to run after them, but they always escape by scampering into some underbrush or a patch of cacti. Since neither animal gets hurt, I let Princess enjoy the thrill of the chase.

People with bird dogs know that their pets want to chase every turkey, roadrunner, or other winged creature that they see. But they, too, are trained for specific birds. A quail dog learns to react only to quail. It properly ignores rabbits, skunks, and even other birds. Such a dog learns to point at the quail and not flush them out until commanded to do so. Quail dogs that fail to learn this discipline are of no use in hunting and will not have the opportunity to do what they were created to do.

If a dog can be trained to act according to its purpose and not get sidetracked, how much more should we learn to live the kind of life God designed for us? As much as we want to pursue the things that will distract us from our purpose, certainly we can learn to look past them and see a better way to live. This is a big message particularly for men, because it is in our nature to chase things that often end up causing harm: food, pleasure, entertainment, sports, hobbies... And, of course, one of the strongest urges of all is women. Not only is it our nature to pursue the wrong things, but such behavior is also fed by a society that embellishes and encourages the fulfillment of every desire.

For example, every boy needs to hear, "Yes, women are beautiful, and we can't help but notice them, but don't chase them." If a boy is properly trained and learns the wisdom of restraint, then he will say, "I've been trained for a purpose, so I am going to look straight ahead and keep my eyes on the proper goal." It is possible to acknowledge the beauty of a woman without being distracted or enticed to go astray.

Every man needs to learn to enjoy pleasure and entertainment without being consumed by it. If a dog can be trained to notice twenty-five different kinds of birds but point to only one, then a man can learn to train every appetite.

God gives us the ability to train our eyes, ears, appetites, and desires so we don't chase after every compulsion or distraction. We never seem to realize the pain these things can cause until it is too late. That is why we must lay down our desires and submit ourselves to training through the Word of God. Only then can we discover our true purpose in life and enjoy the things He has created and given to us without being destroyed by them.

It takes help from God, but it may also require help from others who have been properly trained—by that I mean other Christians—to learn to fix our eyes on His purpose, to press on for the prize of the high calling in Christ Jesus.

> I press on to possess that perfection for which Christ
> Jesus first possessed me. No, dear brothers and sisters,
> I have not achieved it, but I focus on this one thing:
> Forgetting the past and looking forward to what lies
> ahead, I press on to reach the end of the race and receive
> the heavenly prize for which God, through Christ Jesus,
> is calling us. (Philippians 3:12–14)

This is the challenge. Wounds from our past, diversions in our present, and worries in our future will distract us from what really matters. God wants to teach us how to live according to His purpose. He has a glorious prize awaiting each of us if we will simply submit to His will, focus on His purpose for our lives, and act upon it every day.

4

Got a Sticker?

As Princess is busy sniffing and exploring, frequently she steps on a sandbur or, as we say here in Texas, "a sticker." It is the saddest thing to see a little dog that barely has legs pull up one of them so her belly drags the ground. It's pitiful!

With the kindest, most inviting voice possible, I call out tenderly to Princess, "Got a sticker? Papaw will help you." In the most humble fashion, she limps over to me for help. I always remove the stickers, but sometimes they break off and leave a tiny thorn in the pad of her paw. Princess will continue to hobble around until I say, "Let Papaw look."

She gets up in my lap, lies on her back, and puts her paws up in the air. I'll turn on a light, put on my glasses, and sometimes use a magnifying glass. Gripping a pair of tweezers, I will tell her, "Papaw will get it, but it may hurt when I pull it out." After I remove it, she licks her paw for a minute, then she's happy again. She races around in circles, expressing joy and relief.

As I was reflecting on this process, I realized some profound truths. When I can tell that she's in pain, I lovingly invite her into my lap to take care of it. People also need a compassionate invitation in order to gain their trust so they will come for help. Princess would never come to me if I shouted, "Stupid dog. Get out of the yard. Quit sniffing around. You're going to get what you deserve. I told you not to go there!"

That would not make her want to get in my lap. In fact, she would probably run from me! But this is what many children hear from their moms and dads: "Shame on you, stupid child!" This is also what we too often hear within the family of Christ. Believers can be harsh, judgmental, and unforgiving: "I can't believe you did that! You will reap what you've sown!"

Who would want to respond to those kinds of comments?

Jesus didn't call us dogs, but He did say that we are like sheep, and sheep are not the smartest of animals! We are sheep with stickers. Yet Jesus says to us, "Got a sticker? Got an issue? I'll get it out. I'll pour oil on the wound. Let Me help."

The apostle Paul wrote, "God's kindness leads you toward

repentance" (Romans 2:4, NIV). Would someone with a "sticker" come to you for help? What if that "sticker" is same-sex attraction, porn addiction, drug addiction, or something equally devastating? Would you be a safe person from whom to seek help? Would you welcome that individual into your arms and work with him or her to get rid of the pain as well as the source of the pain?

We are all like sheep in that we have strayed from the Shepherd's care. There is no righteous person, not even among believers. There is only One who is perfect, and that's God, so the only goodness in us is godliness, and our only righteousness is Christ in us. God forbid we boast except in the cross (see Galatians 6:14, NIV).

There is power in confession—not in covering up, but in the covering of His grace and the cleansing of our sin. We need one another to find healing. "Therefore confess your sins to each other and pray for each other so that you may be healed" (James 5:16, NIV). This literally means being made whole. Keep in mind, we don't confess our sins, or stickers, to feel better but to be free from the source and be made whole.

Jesus died to redeem us and set us free. We should never feel shame over a battle, because I believe we are not free from battles, but we are free to fight battles and win. Nearly everyone has some kind of sticker, whether huge or small. Maybe you don't want anybody to know. God wants to remove it, even though it may hurt for a short time. Repent while it is still a secret, and let the Lord begin the healing process. Then turn to those around you and invite them into arms of compassion to remove their stickers so they can find healing too.

5

Making God Look Good

One afternoon Princess was playing in our family room, tossing around her squeaky toy, rolling on her back, and kicking her short legs wildly in the air. I grinned as she brought her toy to me, luring me into a game of fetch. Then as I repeatedly flung the toy, I wondered, *Why did God create such an amazing array of animals: some wild and some domesticated, some big and some small, some remarkably beautiful and some almost laughable?*

In my mind and heart, God responded, *So that you, as a human being, can understand how much I, in all My infinite wisdom and omniscient power, could love someone so inferior. If you can love an animal that is obviously inferior and love it with great depth, you might begin to grasp just how much I love you.*

I want you to understand how much pleasure I get from your pleasure, how much concern I have for you and your well-being, and how I desire to give you direction in your life. But most of all, I want you to understand how real and how deep My love is for you.

Wow—what a wonderful insight, and it all started with a little dog and her master enjoying a game of fetch!

Of course, this would all seem ridiculous if I did not first believe in God. If I had a godless view of life in which mankind evolved from random circumstance, and if Darwin's survival-of-the-fittest idea meant that some species reigned over others with no spiritual or moral consequences, then it would make no sense for a superior being to actually love an inferior one. But the way I care for a little dachshund illustrates how a vastly magnificent Creator loves and cares for you and me.

Even through such a simple thing as a pet, God shows Himself to us, if we will only open our eyes and see Him:

For ever since the world was created, people have seen
the earth and sky. Through everything God made, they
can clearly see his invisible qualities—his eternal power
and divine nature. (Romans 1:20)

God lives among us, revealing His character and qualities through this complex world. Despite the corruption of our world, His perfect nature can be found. The Bible tells us that God rescued us from the grip of sin at a great price, that He has a plan and purpose for our lives, and that He trusts us with great responsibilities and blessings. Despite our inferior status to Him, He gives us tremendous opportunities.

> What are mere mortals that you should think
>> about them,
>>> human beings that you should care for
>>> them?
>> Yet you made them only a little lower than
>> God
>>> and crowned them with glory and honor.
>> You gave them charge of everything you made,
>>> putting all things under their authority.
>>> (Psalm 8:4–6)

A dog trainer once told me, "The fact that my dogs are so obedient, responsive, and well trained is not because I want to make the dogs look good. Their response to my commands and direction makes *me* look good."

In a similar way we find fulfillment in life when we cease to draw attention to ourselves and focus instead on magnifying and glorifying our Master, making *Him* look good. Jesus said, "If you try to hang on to your life, you will lose it. But if you give up your life for my sake, you will save it" (Matthew 16:25).

Jesus the Son said to those who saw Him that they were also seeing God the Father. The earthly manifestation of God perfectly reflected God in heaven. This is what Christians are called to be—a reflection of Christ: "Let your light shine before men in such a way that they may see your good works, and glorify your Father who is in heaven" (Matthew 5:16, NASB). Life outside of His purpose lacks meaning. But life in His Spirit is filled with incredible supernatural relationships and events.

The first followers of Jesus recognized the revelation of God through the incarnate Christ and declared His lordship boldly. This upset the religious leaders of the day, who told Jesus, "'Teacher, rebuke your followers for saying things like that!' He replied, 'If they kept quiet, the stones along the road would burst into cheers!'" (Luke 19:39–40).

Creation declares God's glory, but we are meant to live lives of praise, not just with our mouths, but with our entire beings.

Through a yielded life, listening to His voice and obeying His commands, we make God look good. In doing so, we find our place in the grand scheme of space and time. And we are able to experience the same simple joy as expressed through a dog that can run and play at the feet of its master.

6

Good for Goodness' Sake

Princess is really a hound—she loves to hunt. I wish I could know what her nose is telling her. She loves to chase rabbits, lizards, mice, squirrels, and anything else she can pursue. She rides in the pickup truck, staring over the steering wheel, just trying to see something move.

You just say the word "truck," and she jumps and yelps, anxious to get into it, stand in my lap, and peer over the dashboard. She is too cute! Her little eyes stare out the window like an excited child. When we see a rabbit or squirrel, I often let her out to chase it.

One summer Betty and I were away at a retreat where I was speaking to a men's group. Since the schedule was full, I didn't have time for a couple of days to let Princess sniff and hunt outdoors. On the third day, after watching her be so patient, I really could sense her disappointment. A little dachshund can look somewhat like a basset hound when it gets down—she looked so sad! I finally told Betty, "I have to take Princess hunting."

"James, you're tired, and it's hot outside," she said.

"But, honey, she has been so good. I *have* to take her."

Princess had behaved so well, expressing her excitement but never getting what she really wanted. She was a perfect little lady! I began to think about children who often manipulate their parents to get what they want. They do some chores, cleaning up their rooms or helping in the kitchen, because they want to go somewhere, buy something, or do something with their friends. Of course, we parents may play along because we want to see our children have fun, but we understand some manipulation is under way.

Princess has begged plenty of times too, knowing what she wanted. But this particular time was totally different. She was just so good! I had to take her out.

I felt as if God spoke to me clearly and said, *Remember the times when you began to notice that your children were just good? They were doing things well because "good is good." They did things right because "right is right." Do you remember how earnestly you wanted to bless them—to do something special for them because you knew they were being good, not to get something, but just because it is right to do right?*

I think this is what it means to have God's Word "written on our hearts" and not just carried around in a leather-bound book. As I thought about it, God touched my heart and seemed to say, *You know, I saw your children doing this too, and I've one-upped you. I've gone way beyond. Look how blessed they are in their marriages and with their families. They learned to do good not just because they were Robisons or because they had a ministry family and everyone expected them to do what was right. They decided to do what was best because it was best, to do right because it was right. Look what has happened with their choices and their futures. Look at the beautiful children they have and the meaningful relationships they enjoy.*

And now we see our grandchildren doing right simply because it is right.

Sometimes it seems as if it's easier to love a dog than to love people, but if we can love our pets and our children, how much more does God love us? We love it when an animal is faithful to us, but God loves it even more when His people are faithful to Him.

When we do right simply because it is right, our heavenly Father will reward us. He is far more faithful than a dog, a child, or any human being. And He rewards us just because He is good and wants to see us happy.

I took Princess out that afternoon to chase rabbits, and she was as happy as a little dog can be. I shared in her joy too. And I smiled as I understood a little more about God's love for us and His desire to bless us when we live a life of obedience and faithfulness.

7

Responding to the Slightest Sound

Often as I read in my study or watch television in my recliner, I hear a light scratch at the door or a faint whimper. Immediately I stop what I'm doing and move toward the sound. I follow the noise until I find Princess needing to get in or out a door. I hear her plea and open the door for her. I don't act annoyed; I simply respond.

If I am attuned to such a faint call for help, how much more does God listen and respond to our cries to Him? He says that He hears us when we lift our voices out of horrible pits (see Psalm 40:1–2); when we knock on doors, He opens them (see Matthew 7:8); when we seek Him, we will find Him (see Luke 11:10).

As surely as I respond to the insignificant request of a dog, God responds to us, and I don't think He considers our pleas insignificant. He cares deeply about not only our needs but also our interests and concerns. He moves to meet them. As surely as we find satisfaction and pleasure in His response, He finds satisfaction in responding to us. This relationship and fellowship is more meaningful to Him than it is to many of us. He has our interests and needs on His heart and desires us to know the importance of having *His* interests and concerns on our hearts.

It's important to me to respond to our dog. I've wanted to ask Princess, "Do you ever appreciate what I do? When I take you outside or play with you or give you a treat, you don't even bark 'thank you.' You just take it and go."

Of course, it's unreasonable to expect a dog to say "thanks," but I want to be sure that *I* recognize every good and perfect gift that comes from above. I want to live my life as an expression of gratitude to God.

I won't ever hear a "thank you" from Princess, but I will keep responding to her needs and desires. I will continue to find satisfaction in the small things that she does: welcoming me when I come home, pressing me to take her with me when I leave, and nudging me for a pat on the head. I accept the fact that her actions prove her love.

Many mornings I have listened to the birds singing at the top of their lungs. We have a mockingbird that sits on the top of our chimney, and his sounds reverberate down the flue. He seems to imitate every bird in the neighborhood. Actually, he is declaring to every other bird that our chimney is his territory, but as far as I'm concerned, he's whistling praises to God!

I heard the mockingbird echoing the other birds one day and thought, *God, I don't want a bird to outpraise me. If birds can spend each day praising You, I can too. I may not be able to sing very well, but I can still praise You and recognize that all creation gives glory to You.*

Through my praise, I declare my life to be God's territory! I know that when I speak His praises, He hears me. To the Creator of the universe, the sound of one person's praise would seem slight, if not inaudible. Yet God not only hears us; He responds! How amazing is that?

Even more amazing, God doesn't respond only to praise. That's a human characteristic, since we tend to prefer congratulatory, self-serving admiration. Our good and gracious Father also hears our needs and responds to our suffering. In fact, He takes pleasure in responding.

The story of the prodigal son is not just an allegory of a wayward man; it's an illustration of God's attitude toward sinners. "So [the prodigal son] returned home to his father. And while he was still a long way off, *his father saw him coming*" (Luke 15:20, emphasis added).

When we turn toward God, He sees us! Then He rushes to our side just as the father ran to his prodigal son, and He restores us to fellowship with Him. James stated it simply: "Come close to God, and God will come close to you" (4:8). Just the slightest indication that we desire to be near to God is enough for Him to notice and take action. He even wants us to voice our wishes. "Don't worry about anything; instead, pray about everything. Tell God what you need" (Philippians 4:6). Though the answer is always up to His wisdom and providence, He tells us to bring everything to Him.

Sometimes I tell Princess no because I understand that her desires are not in her best interest, but that does not diminish my love for her. Really, it just confirms it. But even when I deny her wish, I hear her and I respond.

We are privileged to have a God who is our Father and friend, who gives far more attention to our needs and desires than I could ever give to a dog.

8

The Dog That Wouldn't Learn

Hershey's owners referred to him as a "handful," and that was putting it mildly. The chocolate-brown poodle mix knew no boundaries. He greeted guests by pouncing on them. If the front door opened more than three inches, he would try to nose his way out. When he made it, he shot down the street as quick as he could. The family of four—mom, dad, and two young daughters—loved him, but he stressed them out. They tried various techniques to train him, but he was stubborn.

Hershey just wouldn't learn.

A grandmother's death required Hershey's family to go out of town. They considered leaving the high-strung dog with some friends but decided against it. He was simply too much trouble. So they put him in their minivan and drove several hours away to attend the funeral. After the service they had to clean out the grandmother's home so they could sell it. The last thing they needed was Hershey under their feet, getting into things and darting through open doors.

They were guests in another family member's home, and they couldn't trust the dog enough to let him run loose, so they locked Hershey in the garage. A cat door led outside, so they barricaded it with several cases of canned soda.

Hershey had everything he needed in the garage: food, water, and a few toys. But that wasn't enough for him. He wanted out. So he chewed through the cardboard, scattered the soda cans, and escaped. He must have thought he had finally found true freedom. But he was in a strange city with nobody to look after him.

Several hours later the family returned to find a mess in the empty garage. The children were distraught. Search parties combed the neighborhood. Hershey was nowhere to be found.

Later that night the family called their home phone to check their voice mail. Sure enough, there was a message about their dog, and the news wasn't good. Hershey had run into a busy street and had been promptly hit and killed by a car.

Whoever hit him didn't stop, but a kind person retrieved the ID tags and called the telephone number. The next morning he brought over all that was left of the poodle: his collar and tags.

Hershey's death made an already difficult situation even worse. Yet nobody was too surprised by his demise. He had a pattern of unruliness and could never be trusted. In the end he destroyed the boundaries that his protectors had put in place, set out on his own, and experienced his tragic fate.

Unfortunately, many people are like Hershey. They strive against the boundaries God has put in place. They are never satisfied with their circumstances and foolishly believe they can find happiness outside of their real safety, comfort, and provision. They destroy the very walls that protect them from harm, and they never consider the pain they cause those who truly care for them. The Bible addresses this:

> Fear of the LORD is the foundation of true
> knowledge,
> but fools despise wisdom and discipline....
> "For they hated knowledge
> and chose not to fear the LORD.
> They rejected my advice
> and paid no attention when I corrected them.

Therefore, they must eat the bitter fruit of
    living their own way,
   choking on their own schemes.
For simpletons turn away from me—to death.
    Fools are destroyed by their own
    complacency.
But all who listen to me will live in peace,
    untroubled by fear of harm."
     (Proverbs 1:7, 29–33)

Hershey was just a dog, so it's easy to understand why he couldn't comprehend the truth about his situation. But people are not much smarter. When we learn to trust God, even when we don't understand the boundaries He puts in place, we can begin to experience the peace and protection He provides. When we cease striving against His commandments and rest in His superior wisdom, we not only enjoy a better life, but we also earn His trust, which leads to greater things.

If Hershey had been more trustworthy and disciplined, he might never have been taken on the trip, or the family might have taken him to the grandmother's house with them. But he had proven himself unreliable. More accurately, he had actually proven himself reliable—they *knew* he would get into trouble!

God gives each of us boundaries—guidelines to keep us safe from harm and rules to discourage us from hurting others. At the same time He gives us a free will. If Hershey's owners had known that he was headed toward death that day, they surely would have tied him up or placed him in a secure cage. But God doesn't put us in cages. He tells us how to live and prosper, then allows us to choose. He laid out His design in the book of Deuteronomy:

> See, I set before you today life and prosperity, death and destruction. For I command you today to love the LORD your God, to walk in his ways, and to keep his commands, decrees and laws; then you will live and increase, and the LORD your God will bless you in the land you are entering to possess.
>
> But if your heart turns away and you are not obedient, and if you are drawn away to bow down to other gods and worship them, I declare to you this day that you will certainly be destroyed. You will not live long in the land you are crossing the Jordan to enter and possess.
>
> This day I call heaven and earth as witnesses against you that I have set before you life and death,

blessings and curses. Now choose life, so that you and your children may live and that you may love the LORD your God, listen to his voice, and hold fast to him. (30:15–20, NIV)

It takes discernment to see the boundaries God places in our lives, and it takes wisdom to live within them. But when we consciously choose to accept His wisdom and submit to His will, we experience boundless joy.

God's rules are designed, not to impede our happiness, but to empower us. His instructions do not bind us; they free us. He desires to save us from unnecessary pain and sorrow.

Let's learn from the tragic mistakes of others and choose to live within God's boundaries, for they bring protection, provision, and peace.

9

The Blind Dog
Helped Me See

While shopping at an office-supply store recently, I witnessed an odd sight. A man was pushing a pink baby carriage down the center aisle of the store. It was smaller than a normal carriage, similar to a doll buggy. I looked into the carriage, and there was a beautiful little dog. He was tiny and had a mane that looked like a lion's. I'd never seen a dog like that! I leaned into the carriage and said, "You sure are cute. You really are pretty."

Then the dog's owner called its name and said, "That's the man who needs to pray for you!"

That caught me off guard.

"I know you," the man said.

"Why do you want me to pray for your dog?" I asked.

"My dog is blind," he answered. "He is five years old and has a retinal disease that is afflicting many dogs throughout the country. They are losing their sight in a very short time. We've actually taken him to a doctor in Boston to have a procedure, but the dog is still blind."

"Sure, I will pray for your dog," I said and dropped down

on my knees in the middle of the store. I laid my hands on the dog's face, turning him straight toward me. Though his eyes appeared perfectly normal, I noticed that they didn't follow my movements. I prayed, "God, bless this little dog. He's such a sweet pet, and his family loves him very much. Please make this little dog well. You can heal this dog's eyes. Jesus, would You heal this little dog's eyes?"

I cupped the dog's face in my hands, affectionately putting my cheek against his face. When I stood up, the man said, "Thank you."

I smiled and said, "You evidently know me and can get a message to me. I would like to know if your dog begins to see. My prayers go with you." I finished shopping and left the store.

Later, as I reflected on the moment, God revealed, *My kingdom was manifest in that store, right in broad daylight. You did exactly what believers should do when they recognize the importance of living with an awareness of kingdom power.*

Prayerfully I asked God about the experience: *Why did that man say I was the one who needed to pray for his dog?*

God impressed upon my heart, *Because he was actually saying to his dog, "That's a man who believes in a God who can do anything for anyone...anywhere...anytime. That's My kingdom!"*

If you are fighting a disease in your family or among your

friends and are under some seemingly unbearable weight, I ask you to agree with this fact: the King is here! His presence and power are all around you as surely as the air you breathe. Ask Him to release His healing power to lift the weight and accomplish His kingdom purpose in and through your life, including those you care about.

Trust Him! Kingdom results are in His hands. We receive the seed in receptive soil, and the light of His life and the water of His Word bring forth beautiful fruit in His garden. No plant strains to yield its fruit; no flower, its blossom. If we yield to the King to bring forth kingdom life, He will not fail. His grace working in us effects remarkable changes. We should live amazed by the power of His presence.

You may ask, "What if I'm not healed physically?" Keep trusting Him and thanking Him for a great work of healing and wholeness His kingdom power can accomplish by shaping your character. This is the greatest healing of all. God provides healing for our souls and for our lives, even when we don't see it in our physical bodies. Jesus stated that the goal is for the works of God to be displayed in our lives. (See John 9:1–3.)

Many people have been healed physically but not spiritually, and, as a result, they still can't clearly see God's kingdom purpose for their lives. Jesus can heal a withered hand, but His greater emphasis is on the need for withered lives to be healed by the power of His abiding presence and kingdom reality.

Jesus really did come to heal the brokenhearted and those who may also have broken bodies. All disease and sickness will be absent in the eternal kingdom that is to come. Absent from that kingdom will also be any potential for illness, temptation, or sin, and there will be no more death. It's no challenge in heaven to overcome an enemy, because there's none to overcome. In this life God desires to make us more than conquerors. He wishes us to be ambassadors, carrying His armor, deflecting every fiery suggestion of the Enemy and all the lies in this present world with the shield of faith.

God's kingdom power really did show up in that office-supply store. It wasn't simply an expression of love from a lover of pets, but it was an expression from the Lover of our souls and our lives. It was the heart of One who cares about every concern we have. His desire is not that we should strive for righteous works on our own but that we would allow Him to work His righteousness in our lives every single day.

10

The Whipped Puppy

A friend of mine had a dog that had been beaten and abused as a puppy. Years later, as an adult dog, he still cowered in the corner when strangers walked into the room. If he approached anyone, it was always with his head down and his tail between his legs.

"Is that dog ever going to get over it?" I once asked.

"I don't know," his owner replied. "I've done nothing but take care of him and treat him well, but he still acts like he's being whipped."

A lot of people are like that. They suffer through some painful situation and spend the rest of their lives unhappy and afraid. Many of them have legitimate reasons: abuse, tragedy, loss. Like Jesus's disciples in the tempest-rocked boat on the

Sea of Galilee, they are understandably shaken by the terrible storm. But even when the rain and waves subside, they never reach the other side.

Paul told the church in Thessalonica that his friend and co-minister Timothy was sent "to strengthen you, to encourage you in your faith, and to keep you from being shaken by the troubles you were going through. But you know that we are destined for such troubles" (1 Thessalonians 3:2–3).

Jesus, too, warned us that trials and tribulations will come our way: "Here on earth you will have many trials and sorrows," He told His disciples. But Jesus followed this warning with a powerful statement: "But take heart, because I have overcome the world" (John 16:33). James, the brother of Jesus, took our difficulties one step further: "When troubles come your way," he wrote, "consider it an opportunity for great joy" (1:2).

Why would a good and loving God allow us to experience pain? And why would He expect us to have joy in the midst of suffering? I see three primary reasons:

First, we live in a fallen world and, therefore, suffer the consequences. Because sin is a part of our earthly existence, we feel the pain of mankind's wrong attitudes and actions. We experience the valley of the shadow of death. Every day we witness the results of sin around the world. People suffer, lives are destroyed, and innocents die. Evil not only exists, but it does exactly what the Bible tells us the Enemy came to do: kill, steal, and destroy. The "trials and sorrows" are clear, which magnifies our need for the One who has "overcome the world."

When our pets get sick, we understand the need for a veterinarian. When we see the suffering of this sinful world, we should likewise understand the need for a Savior, the Great Physician.

Second, suffering can glorify God. Oftentimes, pain can help purify us by removing the sin in our lives. Ask those who have faced a terrible illness if their priorities in life have changed. Most will tell you that many things they once considered important fell by the wayside as the things that God considers important took on new significance. The specter of death can force even the most self-centered people to look heavenward. The suffering of a loved one can bring a family closer. Unfortunately, it often takes a tragic or frightening situation to compel us to love, forgive, or connect with others.

This is not to say that suffering is always the result of someone's sin. When Jesus and His disciples came upon a blind man, one of them asked, "Why was this man born blind? Was it because of his own sins or his parents' sins?" Jesus answered,

"It was not because of his sins or his parents' sins. This happened so the power of God could be seen in him" (John 9:1–3). Jesus then healed the blind man, and many lives were touched by the power of God. Certainly, the blind man had faced a lifetime of difficulties. But in the end, Jesus was glorified through that man's suffering.

Whether pain eradicates sin in our lives or simply allows God's power to be shown, trials and tribulations can serve to bring glory to God. And that, in the end, is a good thing.

Finally, suffering can build godly character. Acts 14:22 says that "we must suffer many hardships to enter the Kingdom of God." If God is a good God—and He is—then how can this be?

Through His prophet Isaiah, God told His chosen people, "I have refined you, but not as silver is refined. Rather, I have refined you in the furnace of suffering. I will rescue you for my sake—yes, for my own sake!" (48:10–11). Refinement is a process that brings out the value in a precious metal by burning off the impurities. God's promise to carry us *through* the fire is not a guarantee that we will be rescued *from* the fire but rather the assurance that we will prevail in Him *in the midst of* the fire. We will overcome, but our clothes may smell like smoke!

Once we understand the potential positive role of suffering in our lives as we live and abide in Jesus, the words of James— "consider it an opportunity for great joy"—begin to make sense. We experience the joy of trusting God and discover the peace that passes understanding. This knowledge allows us to move beyond the permanent status of victim and accept the role of overcomer. We no longer have to cower in the corner or walk with our heads down.

Sadly, too many Christians live like whipped puppies. If Paul and Silas could sing praises in jail (and I don't think they were faking it), then why can't we be happy whatever our circumstances? We cannot be good witnesses for Christ and lights in a dark world when we lack something as basic as happiness.

Consider these promises from the book of Psalms, written by a man who was no stranger to tragedy.

> Weeping may last through the night,
>> but joy comes with the morning. (30:5)

> The righteous person faces many troubles,
>> but the LORD comes to the rescue each
>> time. (34:19)

The LORD directs the steps of the godly.
> He delights in every detail of their lives.
Though they stumble, they will never fall,
> for the LORD holds them by the hand.
> > (37:23–24)

In strictly human terms, we all face situations that could justifiably prevent us from being happy. But through the supernatural power of Jesus Christ, we can overcome any situation. When we do this, we are not victims. We are not whipped dogs but are children of the Most High God. We can be agents of positive change—salt and light in this world. Then we will not only claim to have joy, but we will truly possess a visible and attractive quality: happiness.

11

Living with Tilted Heads

Have you ever noticed that when you speak to a dog, it will often tilt its head to the side as if it is trying to understand you? It's the cutest thing in the world. I have no idea what their brains comprehend, but their body language says, "I'm listening and really trying to understand what you're saying!"

We know that dogs, birds, and a few other animals can match enough sounds to respond to commands such as "sit" or "stay." Pets often seem to know their own names. Yet when we say a similar-sounding word with the same voice inflection, they are easily fooled. You can tell an obedient dog to "stray" with the same tone as "stay," and the dog will not know the difference.

Many people are as uncomprehending as animals when it

comes to hearing the Holy Spirit. We can be tone-deaf to God, even though we know He's speaking to us. We don't know when to "stay" and when to "stray," because we cannot distinguish between that "still small voice" of God and other spiritual influences. In fact, we often cannot tell the difference between a spiritual sound and our own thoughts. Through the prophet Isaiah, God said that people "walk in the way which is not good, following their own thoughts" (65:2, NASB).

When I see a dog tilting its head to the side, yearning to understand the words of its master, I see the posture that we must take with our Master, our Father and our God. We must live with "tilted heads," seeking not only to hear God but also to understand what He is saying. As believers, we must seek to hear and know God's truth but also seek to have understanding.

Solomon, the wisest man who ever lived and the writer of Proverbs, repeatedly said that wisdom that comes from above is understanding. He affirmed the idea that we can gain godly wisdom, if only we will learn to hear.

> Tune your ears to wisdom,
>> and concentrate on understanding.
> Cry out for insight,
>> and ask for understanding.

Search for them as you would for silver;
    seek them like hidden treasures.
Then you will understand what it means to
        fear the Lord,
    and you will gain knowledge of God.
For the Lord grants wisdom!
        From his mouth come knowledge and
        understanding. (Proverbs 2:2–6)

If you want your faith to grow, you must learn to hear. How do you hear? Through the Word of God. In the book of Romans, we are taught that "faith comes from hearing the message, and the message is heard through the word of Christ" (10:17, NIV).

His Word is available for you to read, to study, and to pray for understanding (which comes through the enlightenment of the Holy Spirit). It's easy for most of us to find God's words, which are available in many translations. However, it takes effort to actually *hear* the Word. It is not enough just to listen to the audible sound, like a dog tilting its head at the sound of its master's voice, or just to read the written Word; we must actually comprehend the meaning in order to truly hear. We must understand what Christ is saying to us. I have asked God to help me live with my head continually tilted and with a sincere desire to hear clearly and to understand.

When Betty and I look back over the growth of our three children, one of the most comforting realities is that I continually sought not only to give directions and instructions to our children, but I really did seek to give them understanding. I wanted them to know why it was important for them to stay within the boundaries.

As an example, I wanted them to know why they shouldn't play in the street. It wasn't a matter of Betty or me trying to limit their joy and pleasure but rather to extend it by keeping them out of danger. I'll never forget driving toward our home one day when the kids noticed some pancake-shaped, flattened frogs on the road. They reacted to the gruesome sight, and I said, "See, that's why you don't play in the street!"

Who would have thought that dead frogs could become an illustration to impart understanding to children? But God wants us to comprehend His truth and grasp as much of His nature as possible. As humans, we are limited in our natural abilities, but God is not limited in His supernatural possibilities. Creation bears witness to His truth. We can hear it and live it, but we must live with tilted heads, seeking understanding from God.

12

Be Alert:
There Are Warnings

Nearly every animal has some type of signal to warn others in its group of possible danger. Some warnings are simple, such as the bark of a dog, while others are more complex. Chickadees, for example, use two types of calls: the "seet" call warns of flying predators, such as hawks or owls, and the "chick-a-dee" call warns of predators waiting on the ground or perched on a branch. Researchers believe that the number of "dees" at the end of the call ("chick-a-dee-dee-dee") reflects the size and threat of the predator. The more "dees," the greater the danger.

In West Africa, hornbills and Diana monkeys warn one another of approaching predators. When a monkey sends up the warning about a crowned eagle, which also preys on hornbills, the birds respond. But if the Diana monkey sends out the alert about a ground-based animal, such as a cheetah, the birds ignore it since they can just fly away.

I enjoy watching and photographing white-tailed deer, which get their name from the bright white underside of their triangular-shaped tails. What many people may not realize is that the white tail is actually their warning signal. If a deer suspects danger, it flicks its tail quickly. This puts the other deer on alert without scattering them into the woods. But if a deer detects actual danger, it will put its tail straight up, showing all the white, and it will wave its tail side to side while running for cover.

If you walk up on a herd of white-tailed deer and spook them, you will be greeted with a mass display of white "flags" as they wave good-bye and run away. The white-tailed deer may not be the most intelligent of all the animals, but they are certainly among the most alert.

As Betty and I have watched white-tailed deer, we have been greatly impressed by their keen senses of hearing and smell and their eyes, which detect almost all movement. When they sense something, they come to full attention and focus in the direction of the sound, movement, or odor. They also show great respect for the rest of the deer when they focus on something. In the truest sense of the term, they are "on guard," and their concern and warnings are respected and heeded by all the others.

I find myself often praying for Christians not only to be alert but also to show more respect for the concerns and warnings of others. The Bible is full of warnings for us. The writer of Proverbs cautions that "the lips of an immoral woman are as sweet as honey, and her mouth is smoother than oil. But in the end she is as bitter as poison" (5:3–4). The prophets continually warned the Israelites of the consequences of their disobedience. Paul tells us to be alert because we have an Adversary, and he strongly admonishes us not to grieve the Holy Spirit.

Yet people often have to learn the hard way. Proverbs 19:3

says, "People ruin their lives by their own foolishness and then are angry at the LORD." The secret to a successful, blessed life is not hidden; it's written in the Bible for all to read. But if we ignore the warning signs, we will suffer the consequences.

Situations like adultery, murder, and other blatantly wrong actions are clearly defined in the Bible and in our society's laws as damaging to the human condition. But sometimes we don't realize the possible danger. Every day we face more subtle situations where we could use a good warning sign. In fact, we can face it at church.

Consider some of the doctrine taught in the modern church. The controversial "prosperity message" requires true discernment. First Thessalonians 5:21–22 tells us to "test everything that is said. Hold on to what is good. Stay away from every kind of evil."

While I believe that God is good and wants to bless His children, I do not believe that we dictate the terms of God's goodness. Money is man's standard, not God's. He supplies each of us according to our own needs. For some, wealth may be a curse. Just look at people who have squandered vast amounts of money on foolish or sinful pursuits. I don't believe that God wants us to suffer from a lack of basic necessities— many stories in the Bible tell of God miraculously providing food, water, and shelter—but He may not want all of us to be rich according to the world's monetary standards. He may want us to learn to truly rely on Him for our daily needs.

When God led His people out of Egyptian bondage under Moses, they didn't move directly into the Promised Land. In reality, most of them never made it. Yet even in the desert, He provided for their needs. He gave them manna from heaven but told them not to keep it overnight. They had to rely on God every day. So when I hear someone bragging about their righteousness as measured by their wealth, little white flags wave in my mind's eye. I call it a check in my spirit.

Paul wrote of a time when "we all come to such unity in our faith and knowledge of God's Son that we will be mature in the Lord, measuring up to the full and complete standard of Christ." True discernment requires maturity; maturity requires daily growth.

"Then," Paul continued, "we will no longer be immature like children. We won't be tossed and blown about by every wind of new teaching. We will not be influenced when people try to trick us with lies so clever they sound like the truth" (Ephesians 4:13–14). God certainly does want to bless and prosper us in the truest and purest sense of those words. Blessings come in many forms far beyond the material realm.

His warnings are not a list of dos and don'ts to spoil our enjoyment in life; they are like the birds and monkeys screeching from the heights, "Watch out. That will hurt you!"

God gives us warning signs, both written in His Word and written in our hearts. When we learn to listen and act on His call, we can avoid the dangers that destroy the lives of so many people, and we can instead live in peace, fulfillment, and true prosperity.

13

Trapped!

From the earliest biblical times until this very day, man has trapped animals. Daniel was thrown into a pit of lions, suggesting that those lions had been trapped and placed into the pit for the purpose of devouring lawbreakers or enemies of the king.

America's colonial days were filled with trappers and traders who would capture animals for their furs, meat, or other value. Some traps are somewhat humane, while others are downright brutal, but the end game is the same: a loss of freedom and possibly life.

There are documented cases of wolves, tigers, coyotes, and other animals gnawing off a paw to get out of a trap. As gruesome as that is, even animals know that it's better to escape a trap maimed and alive than to die. Jesus reflected this truth when He said, "If your hand causes you to sin, cut it off. It is better for you to enter life maimed than with two hands to go into hell, where the fire never goes out" (Mark 9:43, NIV). I believe the proper understanding of this verse is for us to consider and recognize the horror and eternal consequences of living in bondage to sinful practices.

Fortunately, Jesus also offers forgiveness from sin so that we don't have to amputate body parts! But the powerful entrapments found in this world are serious. The writer of Proverbs said, "The instruction of the wise is like a life-giving fountain; those who accept it avoid the snares of death" (13:14) and "Fear of the LORD is a life-giving fountain; it offers escape from the snares of death" (14:27).

What are these "snares of death"? There are many kinds, but here are five of the most common:

1. *Love of money.* Those who don't know the Bible often misquote Paul by saying, "Money is the root of evil." But cash is not the problem; an idolatrous heart is the problem, and it often manifests itself in the area of finances. Paul actually wrote, "People who long to be rich fall into temptation and are trapped by many foolish and harmful desires that plunge them

into ruin and destruction. For the *love* of money is the root of all kinds of evil. And some people, craving money, have wandered from the true faith and pierced themselves with many sorrows" (1 Timothy 6:9–10, emphasis added).

Many wealthy people have come from humble beginnings. Those who truly understand the value of wealth know the joy that comes from using their influence and finances to help others. Many hospitals, schools, and charities have been built on the wealth of generous entrepreneurs and businessmen.

You can have wealth and not be trapped by it if fulfilling God's will and His purpose is your top priority.

2. *Lust.* It barely needs mentioning that misdirected sexual attraction has ruined the lives of many people. The truth of Proverbs applies to everyone:

> With persuasive words she [the adulteress] led
> > him astray;
> > she seduced him with her smooth talk.
> All at once he followed her
> > like an ox going to the slaughter,
> like a deer stepping into a noose
> > till an arrow pierces his liver,

like a bird darting into a snare,

little knowing it will cost him his life.

(7:21–23, NIV)

Sexual sin is a powerful trap. Nobody is immune from its lure, but through the power of the Holy Spirit, we can resist all temptation. If we don't resist, we are subject to the death and destruction it brings.

3. *Human fears.* Any fear other than the fear of the Lord, which is healthy, is a carnal fear. "Fear of man will prove to be a snare, but whoever trusts in the LORD is kept safe" (Proverbs 29:25, NIV).

Human fears can be difficult to pinpoint because they exhibit themselves in so many forms. All sorts of mental health issues are rooted in fear. Some of the top phobias, according to psychologists, include the fear of water, fear of flying, fear of heights, fear of storms, and fear of speaking in public! None of these are from God. Neither are the less tangible fears of rejection, relationships, disappointment, or being alone. Any fear can be crippling.

4. *Worldly wisdom.* "Stop deceiving yourselves," Paul wrote to the early church. "If you think you are wise by this world's standards, you need to become a fool to be truly wise. For the

wisdom of this world is foolishness to God. As the Scriptures say, 'He traps the wise in the snare of their own cleverness'" (1 Corinthians 3:18–19).

Thinking we are wise outside of the godly wisdom of the Bible is a form of self-deception. It is a cunning trap, because the victim seldom realizes that he or she is ensnared.

5. *Words.* "The tongue has the power of life and death," the Bible tells us (Proverbs 18:21, NIV). Almost all of us can recall something hurtful that was said to us. If we are not careful, the damaging words of others can prove to be a lifelong trap. How many children have spent their lives cursed by the cruel or foolish words of their parents? How many marriages unravel because of careless words? We must lean on the Word of God, not the words of others, to guide us.

Our own words, too, can become a snare. Proverbs 18:7 says, "A fool's mouth is his undoing, and his lips are a snare to his soul" (NIV). We must be guided by the Spirit every day, because just a few ungodly words from our lips can become our downfall.

Given the damage done by traps, one could wonder why people would ever succumb to them. But the tricky thing about traps is that they don't *look* that bad! Satan is a deceiver, so it stands to reason that he would not present us with something so obviously destructive. At least not on the front end.

When trappers set out to capture an animal, they often bait the trap with something that every animal not only wants but needs: food. Those traps are designed to promise the fulfillment of a basic need or desire. Other traps are simply well disguised. The most rudimentary trap—a pit—is covered so that it appears to be part of the natural environment. The unsuspecting animal simply walks along and falls into a hole in the ground.

Many traps look good or at least harmless at first. It is said that certain monkeys are easily trapped by placing a bunch of bananas in a container with a narrow opening at the top. When a monkey smells the bananas, it reaches through the narrow opening, grabs a banana, and gets stuck. The hunter merely walks up to the monkey and captures it. To be free, all the monkey needs to do is let go of the banana.

Worldly wisdom certainly looks good at first. So do money, lust, power, recognition, and a host of other traps. But when we take hold of these things, we are stuck. We must learn to let go and trust God for everything.

We are not animals. We have access to godly wisdom and do not have to live trapped by the snares of death. When we come to Jesus Christ, He promises freedom.

14

Under His Hand

We have a mat in our garage decorated with a dachshund and the phrase "Caution: Dog Cannot Hold Its Licker." This is especially true when I'm trying to sleep.

If Betty gets up before I do, she will sometimes allow Princess to jump onto the bed while I am still sleeping. Normally my little friend comes straight to my face to show her affection with a wet mess of dog kisses. It's about as shocking as a pitcher of cold water poured on your head!

One morning I felt her jump up on the bed, so I braced for the barrage. It never came. Instead, she thrust her nose under my hand, wanting me to pet her. In a flash I received an impression from God that this is how we should approach Him every morning.

Imagine how our lives would change if our first thought was not *Oh no, another day* or *Am I late for work?* For those who have experienced loss, that waking moment may bring the thought *I wonder where he or she is* or *I miss my loved one.* I have been told that a smoker's first thought upon waking up is often *I need a cigarette.*

But what if our first action every day was more like Princess's that morning when she thrust her head under my hand? What if the first thing we did every day was put our heads under God's hand so He could guide our thoughts and order our steps? Isn't this what the apostle Paul was getting at in this passage?

> Therefore I urge you, brethren, by the mercies of God, to present your bodies a living and holy sacrifice, acceptable to God, which is your spiritual service of worship. And do not be conformed to this world, but be transformed by the renewing of your mind, so that you may prove what the will of God is, that which is good and acceptable and perfect. (Romans 12:1–2, NASB)

When God's hand rests upon our lives, wisdom will enlighten our minds, and integrity will direct our feet. Jesus said that He *is* light, and His light guides our path. When the light moves, we move. Where He goes, we must go. We not only walk in the light, but we freely express the glory of His light through our lives. This is the life of divine direction under His hand.

When Princess showers me with kisses, I appreciate her enthusiasm and affection, but sometimes it's a bit much. But when she pushed her head under my hand, I turned my attention to her and petted her head as I contemplated God's truth. Her move was not bold or boisterous, yet I noticed her. I wanted to care for her needs.

I have no doubt that God never wearies of our enthusiasm and affection, but I also believe that He notices our submission. "Draw near to God and He will draw near to you," wrote James, the brother of Jesus (4:8, NASB). Under His hand there is warmth and intimacy. When we press in toward God, it's like Princess nudging my hand. He responds with divine love. He presses in toward us. This is perhaps the most intimate relationship that mankind can have with our holy God while we are still alive on this earth. It is supernatural and life changing. Under His hand there is security and safety.

If the owner of a cat or small dog encounters a large, threatening dog, the person will immediately pick up his or her pet and hold it close. When the owner holds the beloved pet, the animal is usually safe. With God we are always safe when under His hand. The psalmist declared, "He who dwells in the shelter of the Most High will abide in the shadow of the Almighty. I will say to the LORD, 'My refuge and my fortress, my God, in whom I trust!'" (91:1–2, NASB). In the gospel of John, we are reassured of God's abiding love for us: "My Father, which gave them me, is greater than all; and no man is able to pluck them out of my Father's hand" (10:29, KJV).

One cannot live in the "shadow of the Almighty" without being close. It requires the kind of trust Princess has in me—simple, yet profound. She trusts me completely, even though her limited mind cannot comprehend my plans. She obeys me, for the most part, and her obedience is rewarded with the good things I bring her. I look for ways to give her joy though I am just a man. How much greater is a close relationship with the Creator of the universe when we trust Him completely? The joy He gives surpasses anything we could ever conjure up on our own.

The wisdom, peace, and fulfillment of this type of relationship cannot be fully stated. It must be experienced. Perhaps you did not awaken today seeking to have His hand resting on your head, but you can start now by drawing near, and He will draw near to you. Then tomorrow, and every day thereafter, begin your day by pressing closer to God, submitting your will and quieting your mind. When you truly learn to live this way, you will begin to experience the transforming power of His abiding presence.

15

The Good Greeter

When I come home, regardless of how long I've been away, Princess celebrates my return. She barks her greeting, wags her tail, and follows me until I acknowledge her. Even on the worst days, I can always count on a joyous welcome. Cat owners tell me the same thing. Their pets will rub up against their legs or jump into their laps just to show affection and to gain some in return.

Why can't people be that way?

Paul wrote a whole passage on greetings. In the sixteenth chapter of Romans, he told the believers there to welcome a woman he had sent "as one who is worthy of honor among God's people" and asked them to "help her in whatever she needs" (verse 2). Paul also greeted those in the church, his friends who traveled with him, and the leaders among the Christian community. "Greet each other in Christian love," Paul urged them (verse 16). Another translation says, "Greet one another with a holy kiss" (NIV).

In the early church, believers were anxious to greet their fellow believers. Sadly, in many churches today we hardly acknowledge one another. Even though churches often have greeters at the door, which is a wonderful gesture, they tend to function as doorstops as they are ignored or awkwardly recognized by those passing into the building to worship and, ostensibly, to fellowship.

I think this pathetic response is a by-product of three things in contemporary society. First, we take it for granted that so many people are Christians. During the times of the early church, Christians were a distinct minority. Coming across a fellow believer was not as common as it is for us today, so there was genuine excitement inherent in the meeting. Second, we lack a true bond with other believers, even within our home church. We attend church at weekly intervals (or less) and don't spend the time needed to get to know people. Finally, and perhaps most important, I believe that far too many churchgoers are short on that one vital quality required to connect with others—one that my dachshund exudes every time I come home: *happiness.*

While the explosion of the Christian faith is exciting and, ultimately, the goal of the Great Commission, we must not be so shortsighted that we overlook the great blessing of a community of believers. The pervasiveness of churches should never rob us of the joy of gathering in the name of Jesus Christ. The very fact that we can freely attend a church and worship in a myriad of styles should put smiles on our faces every time we walk through the doors. That alone should make us "greet each other in Christian love." We are amazingly blessed just to be in the presence of other believers, whether it's a small congregation or a megachurch.

The fact that we can be strangers in our home church is a sad reflection on Christianity. Paul's charge to the church in Rome to help his friend in "whatever she needs" should be the calling of every church. Only through the development of real relationships will we be able to discern people's needs and work to meet them. Yet we tend to stand aloof, not wanting to take the initiative and time to invest in the lives of others. This is more damaging than we can ever imagine. Fellowship is a vital part of Christian growth, but many churches miss out on the opportunity to connect.

Have you ever been in a church where people act as if they don't want to be there? I have. From the platform I have gazed out on a congregation that looks as if they've swallowed a curtain rod. They sit sternly in the pew, radiating judgment and misery. If that describes your church, you may need to change churches!

David wrote, "I was glad when they said to me, 'Let us go to the house of the LORD'" (Psalm 122:1). If attending church is not an occasion for rejoicing, something needs to change. Since God looked on Adam and said, "It is not good for the man to be alone" (Genesis 2:18), how can we look on our churches and think, *I don't really need to get to know those people*? Churches can be a wellspring of encouragement, strength, and happiness, but we must step out in courage and faith to get to know one another, which all begins with a greeting.

If you have been bought by the blood of Jesus Christ, saved from the penalty of sin, and baptized into the freedom and fullness of the Lord, then you should radiate happiness. Such a visible joy attracts people. What better place to share that joy with others than at church? So take a cue from our pets, and greet one another with grace, peace, joy, and excitement.

16

Believe and "By Live"

My granddaughter has a Shih Tzu named Max. His favorite thing in the world is a pepperoni-flavored stick that comes in a shiny plastic bag. Max will speak, roll over, jump, or dance for a treat. But the one thing he won't do is dig into the bag for it.

In fact, just to illustrate his fear, my granddaughter once placed the snack on the floor next to the bag and backed away. We watched as the dog shuffled back and forth, whining for the treat and growling at the bag, struggling with the decision of whether to go get his coveted snack or keep his distance from the bag. In the end his fear won, and he gave up on the pepperoni stick.

Max's fear doesn't end with the shiny treat bag. Max is

afraid of most containers—paper sacks, soda bottles, empty cans. If a container holds food, no matter how tempting the smell, he believes it is to be feared. And because he believes it, he lives by it.

Pastor Bill Ramsey Jr., who ministers at a large church in north Fort Worth, says that the word *believe* essentially means "by live." What we really believe is what we will really live by—or at least try. This is not just the case with my granddaughter's dog; it's true for people too.

Cat lovers will tell you how wonderful their pets are. It doesn't matter if they have a Persian, Manx, Siamese, or other popular breed, people who believe that cats are great cannot be swayed. Yet there is an old superstition that if a black cat crosses your path, something bad will happen. Few people believe that today, but those who do carefully avoid cats, especially black ones. They can pretend not to believe the superstition. They can even profess otherwise. But their actions give them away. They won't own a black cat, and they probably feel uncomfortable around those who do. Belief, whether logical or not, drives behavior.

It's easy to say that we believe the Bible, but sometimes it seems difficult to live by it. Which raises the question: What do we really believe? "Examine yourselves to see whether you are in the faith," Paul wrote (2 Corinthians 13:5, NIV). He realized that our beliefs should translate into our thoughts, words, and actions. Otherwise, it raises doubts as to what we really believe. Of course, none of us is perfect, so there is a lifelong struggle to align our old natures with our new spirits. But even that struggle hinges on our true beliefs.

To test your belief system, try this exercise for self-examination. From now on, substitute the phrase *live by* for the word *believe.* Instead of saying, "I believe in daily prayer," say, "I live by daily prayer." If the second declaration is true, then so is the first one. If not, there is a disconnect. For example:

- You may believe in studying God's Word, but do you live by it?
- You probably believe in the fruit of the Spirit: "love, joy, peace, patience, kindness, goodness, faithfulness, gentleness, and self-control" (Galatians 5:22–23). Do you live by such fruit?
- Christians believe in the omnipresence of God. But do you live by the belief that He is with you every moment of the day?
- Most Christians believe in being an unashamed witness for Jesus Christ. Not near as many live by that example.

Jesus said, "If you love me, you will obey what I command" (John 14:15, NIV). In other words, if we *believe* that we love Him, we will *live by* what He asks us to do. How can something so simple seem so hard? Just before Paul told us to examine ourselves, he said that "we are weak in him, yet by God's power we will live with him" (2 Corinthians 13:4, NIV). This natural weakness can only be overcome by a supernatural presence. In a sense, Paul is calling our bluff. It's similar to people who are guilty of animal cruelty yet claim to love their pets. Their actions don't line up with their words.

There has always been criticism of hypocrisy among Christians. Of course, that is true because we hold to a standard that is beyond our own capabilities. If we believed that right and wrong did not exist, I suppose we could escape all hypocrisy. But because we choose to follow God's Word and strive to align our lives accordingly, we often fail and fall short of the standard. This is where the glory lies. Yes, we believe in something that is more wonderful than human nature. Yes, we believe that we can be transformed by the grace of God into better people. And that is why it should be a daily exercise to turn what we "believe" into what we "by live."

For many people, including some Christians, the problem

isn't so much living by what they believe as it is not actually knowing what they believe. If you do not know the Bible and fail to experience God's power in your life, you will not know what to believe. You might as well be afraid of plastic bags! The apostle Paul exhorted, "Work hard so you can present yourself to God and receive his approval. Be a good worker, one who does not need to be ashamed and who correctly explains the word of truth" (2 Timothy 2:15). The King James Version uses the word *study* instead of *work hard*. The point is the same: in order to know the truth, we need to know God's Word.

Too many people believe the wrong things because they do not test them against the Word of God to find out if they're true. We're familiar with the phrase "The truth will set you free," but many people don't know the full context of it. Jesus told those who followed Him, "You are truly my disciples if you remain faithful to my teachings. And you will know the truth, and the truth will set you free" (John 8:31–32).

If Max knew that plastic bags are harmless, he'd be free of an irrational fear. But he's a dog that simply doesn't know better. In a sense, his canine belief system is messed up!

As God's children, we can know the truth, and it can set us free from bad thinking. Through faithful obedience to Jesus's teachings, which comes from a familiarity with the Scriptures and closeness to God through the Holy Spirit, we can develop a correct belief system. We can profess to *believe* the Word of God, but we experience a whole new life when we learn to truly *live by* it.

17

Incomplete Loves

Beth Moore, a wonderful friend and teacher on our television program, *LIFE Today,* has a Border collie named Star. She describes the cherished pet as her "best buddy" and relates a story to illustrate an insightful biblical truth.

Since Beth's ministry has its own office building, she frequently takes Star to work with her. This breed is prone to substantial obsessive-compulsive issues, so they tend to fixate on their owner. In a very real way, Beth "completes" Star. She sleeps in a spot where she can see Beth as soon as she opens her eyes. She puts her head down and tries to herd Beth so that she will go where Star desires. When she accompanies Beth to work, Star stares at her all day while she's working.

Beth's coworkers love Star and consider her the staff mascot. But once, when Beth had to leave the office for a few hours, her staff had some difficulty in baby-sitting the dog. After Beth left, they brought Star to the floor where the whole administrative team works. Star went from office to office, greeting everyone (or perhaps looking for Beth), then began to whine. Nobody could calm or quiet the dog. As Star became more distraught, they became desperate. Finally they tried playing a DVD of Beth teaching. It worked! Star sat right in front of the television, quiet and content. When Beth returned, Star was still fixated on the television screen, watching her master's every move.

That humorous illustration provides insight into human relationships. One of our biggest frustrations in life comes from the incomplete love we experience when we pin our hopes for fulfillment on people, experiences, or things. An incomplete love almost fulfills us but still leaves us yearning for more. These incomplete loves are wonderful gifts from God, but nothing on this planet can truly complete us.

Receiving support from others during difficult times is very healthy. We need it for comfort, affirmation, and, occasionally, healing. This "fellowship of suffering" is a beautiful thing because it connects us with others who have experienced the same sort of pain. You get to know someone well enough that you feel like you can honestly say, "Yes, I totally get that because I've been through every single bit of it!"

However, if you stay close enough to that person, sooner or later you will come to a place of disappointment and departure. You may feel alone at this point because you thought you had found someone who completely understood you. Then you begin to realize that he or she can't go there with you 100 percent because you're processing everything through your own personal history. Only you grew up in your family and felt what you felt and experienced what you experienced.

The Bible says, "Cursed are those who put their trust in mere humans, who rely on human strength and turn their hearts away from the LORD…. But blessed are those who trust in the LORD and have made the LORD their hope and confidence" (Jeremiah 17:5, 7).

Many animals are herd animals. Gazelles on the African plain stick together. Canada geese migrate back and forth together from season to season. Sheep, cattle, and horses find a level of safety, direction, and comfort by sticking together. Yet all of them are still susceptible to predators. If we, as humans, stick together and rely solely on one another, we will eventually fall prey to our enemy, Satan, who always lurks nearby "as a roaring lion" (1 Peter 5:8, KJV). A time will ultimately come when we have to get to the place where it's only you and I and Jesus.

Proverbs 14:10 tells us, "Each heart knows its own bitterness, and no one else can fully share its joy." Nobody else can enter into the intimacy of everything the way Jesus can. A huge part of our emotional well-being comes from reaching this place. We can let a lot of people off the hook for not "being Jesus" to us, for not being able to read our minds or emotions. God is the only One who completely "gets us," because He knows the intimate ways of our minds and hearts; He knows and has seen things that we don't even remember. "For the LORD will go ahead of you; yes, the God of Israel will protect you from behind" (Isaiah 52:12).

This is not to say that we detach from others. God puts people in our lives so that we can journey together, shoulder to shoulder and elbow to elbow, and share experiences. *Koinonia* is a Greek word in the Bible that means "fellowship, sharing in common, communion." Christian fellowship is an important and necessary part of the Christian life, but it's not simply the casual gathering of people in a church building. True fellowship is predicated upon a common belief in Jesus Christ, then enacted in an active pursuit of a common spiritual goal and bond.

It is the shared experience of life as a true follower of Jesus Christ. Philippians 2:1–2 says:

> If you have any encouragement from being united with
> Christ, if any comfort from his love, if any fellowship
> with the Spirit, if any tenderness and compassion, then
> make my joy complete by being like-minded, having
> the same love, being one in spirit and purpose. (NIV)

Koinonia unites believers under the lordship of Jesus Christ and provides the environment to grow spiritually and fulfill God's purpose in our lives. Fellowship is a gift from God, but it is not a substitute for a one-on-one relationship with Him.

Any love outside of God is an incomplete love. Beth's collie may find purpose through her owner, but such fulfillment is not sufficient for humans. Only God can truly satisfy.

18

Don't Feed the Foxes

Occasionally Betty and I are able to enjoy the majestic mountains of Colorado during wintertime. On one visit we noticed signs that cautioned: "Do not feed the foxes."

I have seen a beautiful red fox bounding through the snow, looking for food. Out of compassion I considered tossing some scrap meat where he would find it. After all, it was cold outside, and the fox was clearly hungry. I enjoyed having the beautiful creature around, but I also knew that it was against the law in Colorado to intentionally place or distribute food for most wild animals.

When we asked a resident the reason for the law, we learned that feeding the foxes causes them to become unnecessarily, even foolishly, dependent upon the handouts. They lose their ability to hunt the naturally available food sources. Making a fox dependent on people destroys its stability and potential for a healthy future.

Apparently, this is a really big problem with deer, because the Colorado Division of Wildlife website says, "Some people may feel the deer do not have adequate food sources in the wintertime and believe that supplementing their diets with grain, corn or hay is helpful. In fact, the contrary is true."[1]

The Bible is filled with references to the lessons we can learn from the wild—from the predatory nature of the wolf to the vulnerability of a sheep. We are cautioned to beware of birds of prey, which, unlike vultures, always attack the living. And there are many influences, both in the spiritual realm and the natural realm, that affect our development of life skills to overcome predators. What wisdom is to be learned by not feeding the wildlife in Colorado?

If you have followed Betty and me on our journey over the last few years or viewed our television program, *LIFE Today,* then you are aware that we continually care for the helpless. We help feed the hungry and provide clean water for those who have only contaminated sources. But be assured, once we stabilize a crisis situation and get suffering people back on their feet, our relief workers teach them skills so they can work for their own food. We actually equip those who were once starving with the knowledge and skills to grow their own crops and cultivate farms to feed themselves as well as others in need. At the same time, we encourage them to look to God as their source.

Jesus told us to consider the birds; they don't worry, because God provides for them. Yet if you watch birds, you will see there is not a lazy one in the bunch. They all work from daybreak until sunset. Jesus said, "Don't worry"; He never said, "Don't work!" Even beggars go to work!

It's an interesting challenge to teach both dependency upon God and a strong work ethic. However, Jesus clearly laid out the principle in a story He told:

> Again, it will be like a man going on a journey, who called his servants and entrusted his property to them. To one he gave five talents of money, to another two talents, and to another one talent, each according to his ability. Then he went on his journey. The man who had received the five talents went at once and put his money to work and gained five more. So also, the one with the two talents gained two more. But the man who had received the one talent went off, dug a hole in the ground and hid his master's money. (Matthew 25:14–18, NIV)

You remember how the story ended. The master eventually returned and learned that two of the servants had invested well and had increased the number of talents. The master was pleased with them. But the third servant—the one who had buried his one talent—was severely reprimanded by the master: "You wicked, lazy servant!... Take the talent from him and give it to the one who has the ten talents. For everyone who has will be given more, and he will have an abundance. Whoever does not have, even what he has will be taken from him" (Matthew 25:26, 28–29).

Here we see two principles at work. Notice that the talents (units of money) came from the master: God is our one true source, and any other source is counterfeit. Next we see that God expects us to use the resources He entrusts to us to build and expand. If we squander or sit on what God has given us, not only will we not be trusted with more, but we will also lose what He has given us.

For decades in America we have been creating a dependent society that believes it is owed a living by productive citizens. Some people are angry at those who are successful (unless they happen to be entertainers or athletes) and fully expect to be taken care of by them. Too many people don't have the will to work and wouldn't accept a job they considered low paying or beneath their dignity. Those who depend on the government, or any source other than God, are buying into a lie. Even those who work hard but do not acknowledge God as their source cannot experience the "joy of the LORD" (Nehemiah 8:10).

I grew up with the poorest of the poor. The majority of places I lived could not be called houses. They were shacks that faced other ugly dwellings or dirty rivers. One was literally on a garbage dump. I never looked around and resented the people who had something better, and I never waited for them to take care of me. Even as a fatherless boy, I decided that if others could make it, I could too. I didn't see a limit to my opportunities as many did where I lived. I saw possibilities. At twelve years of age, I went to work six or seven days a week for pay way below minimum wage. It didn't hurt me one bit. In fact, it helped me!

Later, as a teenager, I came to know the Lord and realized that He was my source. By this time I already possessed a strong work ethic. I wish I could say I have never faltered. But it is easy to become self-sufficient, which is really a form of arrogance. And when the circumstances of life put us in a financial bind, we may feel like a fox in the winter, hungry for any scrap of food. But if we persevere, knowing God is our source, and continue to work hard, God promises us that He "will supply all

[our] needs according to His riches in glory" (Philippians 4:19, NASB).

We don't feed the foxes in Colorado, because they must learn that God has provided all they need in nature, but it is up to them to learn how to forage for food, even when the snow is deep and the temperature frigid. And if the Lord takes care of the lowly foxes, how much more will He take care of us?

19

Baby Rattlesnakes

Having spent a fair amount of time in south Texas, I have learned the danger of the diamondback rattlesnake. These fierce and powerful snakes can grow more than six feet long and surpass a full-grown man's arm in diameter. Whether walking through tall grass or sleeping in a cabin, one has to be constantly on the alert for rattlers.

What most people don't realize is that the bigger rattlers generally pose less danger than the smaller, younger ones. More mature snakes have developed a sense for the creatures that will threaten them versus the ones that will avoid them. Most animals know that when a rattlesnake "pops" its rattle, it's time to leave the scene. The snakes learn this too, so they signal their warning and wait for the interloper to flee.

Young rattlers, however, don't know which threat is real and which is not. Out of fear, they may strike anything that comes near. Younger ones also have not learned to control the amount of venom released with a bite, so they typically hit their victims with a full dose. These two factors make baby rattlesnakes more dangerous than the big ones. Yet, if given the option to kill one of two snakes, most people would reflexively target the larger one. It's easy to think, *Oh, that's just a small snake. It can't hurt as much.* That mistake can lead to a lot of pain.

Sin is like that too. People tend to look at the "big" ones, such as murder, adultery, or theft, and ignore the "small" ones, such as pride, bitterness, or envy. This tolerance of the "small snakes" leads to a lot of pain. Just because something isn't out in the open or punishable by law doesn't mean it can't destroy a life. To the contrary, the sins that tend to go unnoticed can be the most poisonous to our souls.

After receiving a hip replacement, I contracted a terrible staph infection. *Staphylococci* can commonly be found in the nose and on the skin of healthy adults. Normally, the bacteria do not cause disease. But injury, damage to the skin, or, as in my case, a serious surgical procedure may allow the bacteria to overcome the natural protection of the body. The resulting infection can range from mild to severe and can even be fatal.

Mine was pretty bad. I spent several days in the hospital and had weeks of treatment. The antibiotics lasted for months—all to kill bacteria invisible to the naked eye. This tiny microorganism could have cost me my life.

During the battle with a staph infection, I found myself recognizing how suddenly an unwelcome enemy can strike. While I was bedfast, God took me back to Isaiah 58. In this passage God told the listeners and His chosen family of faith that if they would heed what He said and practice His commands, they would become a "well-watered garden" and an "ever-flowing spring" (verse 11).

God revealed to me that in the comfort and fruitfulness of my own Christian life and ministry, I had tolerated baby rattlesnakes in God's garden. One example was my appetite for food, especially sugar, which was damaging me physically, leading to borderline diabetes and hindering my battle with infection. Rather than me controlling my appetite, my appetite controlled me.

I was also undisciplined in getting regular exercise, excusing myself because of my damaged right hip. The heavenly Father let me know that I must be very concerned about any issue He sheds light on and that I must get that intruder out of His garden. If the Holy Spirit points it out, get rid of it, because it has the explosive potential of a baby rattlesnake...or staph infection. He revealed to me that I was often distracted from Him and needed to refocus, heading straight toward His standards.

If He sheds light on something in our lives, we are to be as concerned about it as He is—not just the "big" snakes, but the "little" ones too. Every sin in our lives must be eradicated so we can live in fullness and peace.

20

―――⧫―――

Strays

Nothing is more pathetic than stray animals. We've all seen them—a haggard dog on the side of the road, a wild-eyed cat digging through a garbage can. According to the ASPCA, there are approximately 75 million pet dogs and 85 million pet cats in the United States. While it is impossible to determine the number of stray dogs and cats, estimates for just stray cats "range up to 70 million."[2]

The National Geographic Society recently reported an alarming and bizarre phenomenon in Florida. Pythons have invaded the Everglades, flourishing in the warm, moist environment. Apparently, Americans import them as pets, but when they tire of them, they release them into the wild, where they find an abundant food supply. Now the pythons are at

the top of the food chain—along with alligators—and prolif-
erating, which is causing problems for people all over the south-
ern part of the state.

Unfortunately, it is human nature to become fascinated
with something new but grow weary with the responsibility
and daily effort it takes to maintain it. Then the novel thing is
abandoned, whether it's a dog, cat, or python.

Someone in our neighborhood put out cat food for several
feral cats in the area. The strays would drop by, eat the food, then
wander back to wherever they lived. While meaning well, the
homeowners were not really caring for the cats. They treated
them as unwelcome guests, putting out a token dish, but not
taking in the animals as their own. In truth, the cats probably
couldn't have been tamed, but whether they wanted a home or
not, our neighbors were not obliging. They were happy to let
them roam around but not interested in rescuing them.

It's possible to do this in our spiritual lives too. Christians
can treat God like a stray. Like our neighbors with the feral cats,
we may give God a token gift when it's convenient but never
invite Him in. Sure, let God visit, but stay? Not a chance. That
requires giving up some things, taking on responsibility, and
admitting ownership in the relationship. But God is not looking for a place to visit; He is looking for a place to live.

This was precisely the problem with the church at Ephesus, which we read about in the book of Revelation:

> I have this complaint against you. You don't love me or each other as you did at first! Look how far you have fallen! Turn back to me and do the works you did at first. If you don't repent, I will come and remove your lampstand from its place among the churches. (2:4–5)

The Old Testament has a repeated story line of God's people treating Him like a stray. Generations embraced the Lord, then walked away. Even so, God remained faithful to them: "For the LORD your God is a merciful God; he will not abandon you or destroy you or forget the solemn covenant he made with your ancestors" (Deuteronomy 4:31). Jesus echoed this sentiment when He said, "I am with you always, even to the end of the age" (Matthew 28:20).

However, it is possible for people to reject the abiding presence and control of the Holy Spirit. Christians can be overcome with apathy, anger, depression, or other negative emotions. They cease being a light in the world, as if their "lampstand" has been removed.

While I see no scriptural basis to imply that people can lose their salvation, believers can certainly stop producing spiritual fruit. Like the fig tree that Jesus cursed for not bearing fruit, people can dry up spiritually. That tree was still a fig tree, but it had ceased to function according to its ability and purpose.

This can also be observed in churches around the world. Places that once hosted influential revivals are now spiritually dead. The peace, power, and joy have vanished. Churches and other great institutions can become hollow shells if they allow the Lord to visit but do not allow Him to dwell there permanently.

We treat God like a stray animal when we don't allow His presence to dominate our lives every minute of the day. When we insist on being in charge, we remove His Spirit from the throne. The first of the Ten Commandments addresses this directly: "You must not have any other god but me" (Exodus 20:3). Anything that takes precedence for us over God's will, purpose, and direction becomes a god (with a lowercase *g*). It's been said many times but is still true: "If Jesus Christ is not the Lord of all, He is not the Lord at all."

> I am the vine; you are the branches. Those who remain
> in me, and I in them, will produce much fruit. For
> apart from me you can do nothing. (John 15:5)

I like the word *remain* in that passage. It's not a part-time position; it's a constant condition. This is the opposite of treating God like a stray. It means allowing Jesus Christ into every area of our lives, giving Him access to the deepest, darkest places so He can take permanent control.

21

⟡

The Short Life
of the Mayfly

With rod and reel in hand, I love spending time near serene mountain lakes and gently flowing rivers. Trout are the most common fish in these settings, and the most exciting way to catch them is with an imitation fly.

The graceful motion of fly-fishing, with the fisherman whipping the line back and forth in a wide arc, emulates an insect landing on the water and taking off again. While people are familiar with this activity, many don't know the story of the most popular insect model for fly-fishing: the mayfly.

Mayflies live only a day or two as adults. They form in the water, then emerge, molt, and fly around to mate, place their eggs back in the water, and die. Fishermen consider them God's gift to fish because they float or buzz around lakes and streams in abundance, providing ample food. This is also why imitation mayflies make great bait. Splashing them on the surface mimics such a familiar food source that fish naturally strike.

To us the life span of a mayfly seems short, but in the scheme of eternity, our life spans are just as short as the mayfly's. Psalm 90:12 says, "Teach us to realize the brevity of life, so that we may grow in wisdom."

According to the Bible, the realization that life is short is not morbid but wise. Writers in both the Old and New Testaments pondered this idea. Regarding His chosen people, the psalmist reflected:

> Yet he was merciful and forgave their sins
>   and did not destroy them all.
> Many times he held back his anger
>   and did not unleash his fury!
> For he remembered that they were merely
>   mortal,
>   gone like a breath of wind that never
>   returns. (78:38–39)

God understands the significance of our lives, regardless of their lengths. Whether our lives last a few short years or a hundred, He has a plan for each of us. It's our responsibility to seek His plans for us and strive to achieve them.

"How do you know what your life will be like tomorrow?" the writer of James asks. "Your life is like the morning fog—it's here a little while, then it's gone. What you ought to say is, 'If the Lord wants us to, we will live and do this or that'" (4:14–15).

People have forever asked the question, "Why am I here?" The answers to that question are found in the Bible. The reason for our creation can be summed up in two words: God's pleasure.

> Even before he made the world, God loved us and chose
> us in Christ to be holy and without fault in his eyes.
> God decided in advance to adopt us into his own family
> by bringing us to himself through Jesus Christ. This is
> what he wanted to do, and it gave him great pleasure.
> (Ephesians 1:4–5)

> You are worthy, O Lord our God, to receive glory
> and honor and power. For you created all things,
> and they exist because you created what you pleased.
> (Revelation 4:11)

This should give us a tremendous sense of significance. Though for thousands of years, many billions of people have lived on earth—and we each occupy a single life with a relatively short span—God is pleased with us as His creation! Once we understand this awesome truth, the question no longer has the sense of "what's the point?" It is now asked more from the perspective of "what is my purpose?"

Some would argue that individuals have little or no real

purpose: "We live; we do whatever we do; we die. In the end it doesn't matter!" But if God has purpose for a mayfly, how much more purpose does He have for you?

> "For I know the plans I have for you," says the LORD.
> "They are plans for good and not for disaster, to give
> you a future and a hope. In those days when you pray,
> I will listen. If you look for me wholeheartedly, you will
> find me." (Jeremiah 29:11–13)

God has a plan for you! To believe anything else is to believe a lie. There is no question that God created you for His pleasure and for a distinct purpose. Those issues are settled.

The question then becomes, "What is my specific purpose in life?" We must become like David, who said, "I cry out to God Most High, to God who will fulfill his purpose for me" (Psalm 57:2).

There are many nice sentiments about life's purpose. "Live life to its fullest." "Be true to yourself." "Be a good person." All those things are pleasant, and there is a shred of truth in each of them, but they are not the final goal. Jesus said, "For it is my Father's will that all who see his Son and believe in him should have eternal life. I will raise them up at the last day" (John

6:40). Ultimately, the purpose in life is eternal life—finding it ourselves, then taking it to a dying world. Once we receive Jesus Christ, our purpose relates to the Great Commission.

> Therefore, go and make disciples of all the nations, baptizing them in the name of the Father and the Son and the Holy Spirit. Teach these new disciples to obey all the commands I have given you. (Matthew 28:19–20)

It is to this end that we are placed here on earth. We operate in various capacities (apostles, prophets, evangelists, pastors, teachers) and with various gifts (prophesying, serving, teaching, encouraging, caring for others, leading, governing, showing mercy), but the goal is the same (Ephesians 4:11; see Romans 12:6–8). "There are different kinds of service," Paul wrote, "but we serve the same Lord" (1 Corinthians 12:5). We know God created us for a purpose. We are a significant part of His plan. The challenge for each of us is to ask, "How do I fit?"

There's no broad answer for everyone. It requires sensitivity to the Holy Spirit, daily commitment, and diligent devotion. "So be careful how you live. Don't live like fools, but like those who are wise. Make the most of every opportunity in these evil days. Don't act thoughtlessly, but understand what the Lord wants you to do" (Ephesians 5:15–17).

In contrast to the mayfly, our purpose on earth is more than living briefly. It's living fully—fully in God's presence to fulfill His plan for each of us. So live each day to its fullness for His glory.

22

The Woodsman
and the Wolf

A favorite animal fable of mine gives us an intriguing insight into redemption.

A woodsman stumbled upon a wolf caught in a bear trap. "Looks like you're stuck," he said.

"Get away from me," the wolf growled. "I'll be fine."

"You're caught," the woodsman pointed out, "but I can get you out. You just have to trust me."

"Why should I trust you?" the wolf asked. "You're a man, and this trap is man-made."

"The man that made that trap wants to kill you," the woodsman replied. "But I came to set you free. Just let me close enough to open it."

The woodsman put down his ax and took a step toward the wolf.

"Get back!" the wolf snapped. "I see that ax. I know what you do; you cut down trees and destroy the forest. You are a menace!"

"Actually, I planted these trees to harvest for good use. And for every tree I cut down, I plant seven more. But that's beside the point. You're caught, and I'm the only one who can get you out. Otherwise, you'll die there."

"I don't think you can," the wolf challenged. "How do I know you're not lying?"

"Have you never heard another animal talk about my work?" he asked. "I have been setting wolves and others free for years. There are old, rusty traps all through the woods, but I am destroying them one by one. Surely you've heard stories."

"Rumors, yes," the wolf admitted. "But why you? What's so special that makes you the only one?"

The woodsman looked around. "See those birds in

the trees?" he asked. "They can fly, but they are far too weak to help you."

"A deer came by and said he would help me," the wolf said. "He went to get some other deer to help him."

The woodsman chuckled. "That's kind of him; I'm sure he means well. But no matter how many deer he brings, they lack the power to crack open that trap. Their hooves and horns are inadequate to pry the metal jaws apart."

The wolf pondered his position. He knew it was painful and potentially fatal, but he didn't want to trust the woodsman.

"Listen, I'm telling you the truth. If the owner of that trap comes back, you're in real trouble. But if you will just allow me to set you free…"

"I will get out on my own," the wolf snarled. "I don't need your help."

Saddened, the woodsman picked up his ax. "If you change your mind before you die, call out my name, and I will save you." With that, he walked away.

This sad tale is analogous to the way many people respond to Jesus Christ. He is the only One who holds more power than death, and He came to set us free. We are all trapped, and there is only One who can get us out.

Do you want to live? Trust Jesus Christ! He said in John 14:6, "I am the way and the truth and the life. No one comes to the Father except through me" (NIV). Not only does He know the way; He *is* the way.

A lot of people want to argue. They want to convince you that anyone can save you or that perhaps you can even save yourself. Some will tell you that it doesn't matter what you do because nobody "gets out alive," that we're all trapped on this earth until we die! A few will tell you that you're not trapped, despite your deep pain and inability to move.

If you don't think this world is trapped, just look around. Death and destruction are at your door. Evil abounds. Nobody is immune from pain. The real question is this: Who is Jesus Christ? Is He really the Savior, or is He a fraud? Perhaps He was just a nice guy who didn't really know what He was talking about.

C. S. Lewis addressed this in *Mere Christianity* when he pointed out that Jesus was either lord, liar, or lunatic. If He was just a delusional cult leader who merely believed He was God, then He was crazy, and we need not bother with Him. If He was a crafty, egocentric deceiver, then He was more like the devil than God and must be exposed. But if He was neither of these, then He can only be what He claimed to be—the Son of God sent to make a way for us to live eternally with our heavenly Father. He lived a perfect life, setting the matchless example while conquering sin and the grave. If He is who He says He is, then it's not arrogant or cruel to say that He's the only One who can set us free. Instead, it's merciful, truthful, and grace-full.

In this trap called Earth, we must all decide: Who is Jesus? Obviously, the best way to answer that question is to get to know Him. We do that by reading His words, attempting to dialogue with Him, and talking to others who know Him (although this can provide mixed results, since people are fallible).

We don't know how much time we have on earth, so it's urgent that we decide whether to trust Jesus or rely on ourselves or something else. If Jesus really is like the woodsman, then we must trust Him to release us from the trap. Otherwise, we discard Jesus as crazy or deceitful. If we choose not to follow Him, we can't blame Him when we find ourselves dying in a trap from which we can't escape. And we can't call Him unkind or unmerciful when other people don't listen to Him. His offer is clear, but it's our choice to allow Him to do His work.

I believe that Jesus Christ is the real deal. He knows the woods (our world), the traps (sin), and the only way out (Himself). I have trusted Him, and He has set me free.

What about you? Have you trusted Him to set you free?

23

Drunk, but Not on Wine

I n recent years several frightening and bizarre cases of bird deaths have alarmed people around the world. In Vienna, Austria, dozens of songbirds fell from the sky, prompting rumors of the deadly bird flu.[3] In Portland, Oregon, fifty-five robins suddenly dropped dead within a few nearby backyards.[4] At Atlanta's international airport, one of the busiest in the world, cedar waxwing birds were causing myriad problems. "There were these little birds that kept flying around and acting crazy. They were flying all over the entrance road and disturbing people as they drove into the airport," said the environmental compliance manager at the airport.[5]

Despite speculation about disease or even paranormal

activity, the results of bird autopsies all revealed the same thing: the birds were drunk!

In Austria, the livers removed from the dead birds showed so much damage from drinking that "they looked like they were chronic alcoholics," according to a spokesperson for Vienna's veterinary authority. Weather patterns, especially cold snaps late in the spring, allowed ripe berries to stay on the shrubs or trees longer and ferment. Some birds died of ethanol poisoning while others "flew while intoxicated" and broke their necks after smashing into windows and other solid objects.[6]

We live in a day when people are out of control and often under the sway of powerful adversarial influences. God spoke clearly about this through the prophet Isaiah:

> They become drunk, but not with wine,
> they stagger, but not with strong drink.
> (29:9, NASB)

Through the prophet, God asserted that powerful, controlling forces in the spirit realm were influencing the nation of Israel, His chosen people. Isaiah used the analogy of those who stagger and stumble under the debilitating influence of alcohol, like the birds, to illustrate the control that spiritual forces can have over people.

The story of Israel is the narrative of a people freed from Egyptian bondage (a metaphor for any bondage to the world's mentality) and led toward blessings and freedom in the Promised Land. But even though they were physically liberated, their minds were plagued by fear and unbelief. Consequently, they wandered in circles for forty years, then finally the faithful few who believed the truth entered the Promised Land and defeated their enemies through the supernatural power of God. Centuries later the same chosen ones, because of their disobedience to God, became prisoners again (see Nehemiah 9:36).

This slavery-freedom-slavery scenario is repeated today among many in the church family. These believers live in as much or more bondage as they did prior to their deliverance from the world. The enemies in the spiritual realm are called "principalities" and "rulers of the darkness" by the apostle Paul (Ephesians 6:12, KJV). These demonic forces can deceive and captivate even the most influential members of the body of Christ.

Isaiah went on to say that truth cannot be understood because people draw near to God with their words and honor

Him with their lips, but their hearts are far from Him (see 29:11–13).

Much of the church and many in our country are trapped by a spirit of mechanical repetition regarding truth. Prayers are offered, but often they are merely insincere collections of words that go no higher than the ceiling. We sing songs but have forgotten their messages. We go through the motions of worship but live in defeat. We hear sermons but seldom apply them. We have become hearers and not doers of the Word.

Again, God spoke through Isaiah to His people, calling them to repentance and promising them freedom:

> Therefore, please hear this, you afflicted,
> Who are drunk, but not with wine:
> Thus says your Lord, the LORD, even your
>   God
> Who contends for His people,
> "Behold, I have taken out of your hand the
>   cup of reeling,
> The chalice of My anger;
> You will never drink it again.
> I will put it into the hand of your tormentors,

Who have said to you, 'Lie down that we may
walk over you.'
You have even made your back like the ground
And like the street for those who walk over it."
(51:21–23, NASB)

God said to His people and to those with "ears to hear" but who refused to receive the message that they would reach a point of intoxication by the spirit of deception, distraction, and defeat and the enemies of life and freedom would command them to lie down while tormenting forces walked over them as trampled ground. Drunken birds end up with broken necks; people intoxicated by evil end up with broken spirits. But salvation also is revealed in the words of the prophet Isaiah:

Awake, awake,
Clothe yourself in your strength, O Zion;
Clothe yourself in your beautiful garments....
Shake yourself from the dust, rise up,
O captive Jerusalem;
Loose yourself from the chains around your
neck...

"You were sold for nothing and you will be
redeemed without money." (52:1–3, NASB)

Redemption and freedom come through the precious blood
of the Lamb. That goes not only for gentiles but also for every
Jew. The true Zion is the restored, redeemed, blood-bought
people of God. And we can deliver the good news. We can announce peace. We can announce salvation. We can say to Zion,
"Our God reigns…not only in word but also in deed."

As watchmen, we can lift up our voices. We can shout joyfully together, and then the world will see with their own eyes
when the Lord restores a broken life. Jesus promised that those
who become controlled by His spirit, rather than being intoxicated on the things of this world, will be overcomers and will
trample the Enemy under their feet.

24

❈

A Joyful Noise

When those of us who are urban dwellers leave the city and head for the country, we may be surprised at just how noisy nature is! Birds continually sing their songs. Insects join in the chorus. The wind wails. Running water babbles over the rocks in a brook. All these sounds mingle to make a symphony that attests to the wondrous glory of our Creator.

If you have been in church for very long, you have probably heard someone say, "The Lord inhabits the praises of His people." Those words are derived from the King James Version translation of Psalm 22:3, which says, "But thou art holy, O thou that inhabitest the praises of Israel."

This translation can be viewed in different ways. One

interpretation would be that when we sing songs to the Lord, He shows up. Or, when understood cynically, it could mean that a narcissistic God just enjoys hearing mankind heap compliments upon Him.

It's interesting to note that none of the modern translations uses the phrase "inhabits the praise"—not even the New King James Version. Plus, when read in the context of David's psalm, the statement takes on a different meaning.

> My God, my God, why have you abandoned
>   me?
>   Why are you so far away when I groan for
>   help?
>   Every day I call to you, my God, but you do
>   not answer.
>   Every night you hear my voice, but I find
>   no relief.
>
> Yet you are holy,
>   enthroned on the praises of Israel.
> Our ancestors trusted in you,
>   and you rescued them.
> They cried out to you and were saved.

They trusted in you and were never dis-
graced. (Psalm 22:1–5)

This is a psalm of salvation. David's world is crashing in, and he does not feel God's presence, yet he acknowledges the truth that God is ever faithful. The line about the Lord being "holy, enthroned on the praises of Israel" does not elevate God into some unfamiliar position. It is recognition of the character of God and a proper positioning of the psalmist in light of that truth.

David is not saying, "Lord, I think You're so great that I'm going to lift up Your name." He is saying, "God, I can't make it on my own. I realize that You are my only hope, and I know I can depend on You because You are mighty."

Later in that passage David gives thanks for God's inter-vention and ties that salvation directly to his praise.

O Lord, do not stay far away!
You are my strength; come quickly to my
aid!…

I will proclaim your name to my brothers and
sisters.

> I will praise you among your assembled
> people. (Psalm 22:19, 22)

When Captain Chesley "Sully" Sullenberger miraculously landed a debilitated Airbus A320 on the Hudson River, sparing the lives of all 155 people on board, he was naturally the object of much praise—and rightly so. Everyone on the airplane understood that if it hadn't been for his heroic actions, they would have died that day. Nobody had a problem acknowledging his role or voicing their thanks and adoration.

The same is true when we come to realize that without the gracious salvation extended to us by our holy God, we would perish. In that respect, praise does not change God as much as it changes us. It is not a repositioning of His status; it is a repositioning of our hearts.

For the people on that US Airways flight, praising the pilot who saved their lives came naturally. Likewise, praise should come naturally for those of us who partake in the salvation of God.

> I will thank the LORD because he is just;
> I will sing praise to the name of the LORD
> Most High. (Psalm 7:17)

Shout with joy to the LORD, all the earth!
>   Worship the LORD with gladness.
>   Come before him, singing with joy.
Acknowledge that the LORD is God!
>   He made us, and we are his.
>   We are his people, the sheep of his pasture.
Enter his gates with thanksgiving;
>   go into his courts with praise.
>   Give thanks to him and praise his name.
For the LORD is good.
>   His unfailing love continues forever,
>   and his faithfulness continues to each
>   generation. (Psalm 100)

Of course it is much easier to praise the Lord for His salvation and provision when things are going well. But true praise sees past our present circumstances. If it didn't, it would be as meaningless as a conversation on a bad telephone line—on again, off again—and completely pointless. David understood this, which is why, despite his dire circumstances, he chose to praise the Lord.

Paul and Silas understood this as well. When they were locked in the Philippian jail, they didn't gripe about their unjust circumstances. They looked beyond their captivity and saw eternal freedom, so it was natural for them to break out in song. "Around midnight Paul and Silas were praying and singing hymns to God, and the other prisoners were listening" (Acts 16:25).

I like the last part of that sentence: "and the other prisoners were listening." I suspect that the other prisoners didn't like their circumstances either. I imagine a few of them had given up on ever being free again. While the Scriptures don't tell us the words Paul and Silas sang, it is not too much of a stretch to think that they were singing about God's salvation.

Imagine if they were singing a psalm:

> I will praise the LORD at all times.
>> I will constantly speak his praises....
> In my desperation I prayed, and the LORD listened;
>> he saved me from all my troubles.
> For the angel of the LORD is a guard;
>> he surrounds and defends all who fear
>>> him. (Psalm 34:1, 6–7)

The ensuing earthquake that opened the doors to the prison would be enough to make the most hardened unbeliever say, "What must I do to be saved?" That is, of course, exactly what the Philippian jailer said (see Acts 16:30)!

For believers who fully understand their salvation, praise is a natural expression. We praise the Lord for His mercy, love, provision, and wisdom. We praise Him because He is worthy. We praise Him because, like the birds singing their songs, we cannot *not* praise Him.

> Holy, holy, holy is the Lord God, the
>   Almighty—
>   the one who always was, who is, and who
>   is still to come. (Revelation 4:8)

25

‑‑‑✦‑‑‑

Chasing Cars

When our children were young, we got a longhair dachshund named Heidi. She was a beautiful red-headed favorite of the kids. They essentially grew up with her, playing with her after school and traipsing with her through the creek and woods near our house. She was a sweet dog but had a bad habit: chasing cars.

One day she "caught" a jeep driven by my son-in-law in the pasture behind our house. He felt the bump and heard the yelp. Shocked and saddened, he jumped out of the vehicle and found Heidi in a lifeless heap. She had finally caught what she'd been chasing her whole life...and it killed her.

How many people are like that? They pursue wealth, fame,

power, or other seemingly promising things, and when they finally catch them, they suffer unexpected consequences. Unprincipled, self-serving ways always lead to destruction. Some people do not believe that they will reap what they sow, and "claiming to be wise, they instead became utter fools." This passage in the Bible goes on to say, "God abandoned them to do whatever shameful things their hearts desired" (Romans 1:22, 24).

God loves us, just as our family loved Heidi. Many times we chased her to catch her before she caught a car, but in the end her foolish impulses were her downfall. Likewise, God warns us of the consequences of foolish decisions but allows us the free will to choose as we wish, even when it means we'll suffer the consequences. The entire Bible is a handbook to life, but we have to follow its advice.

Jesus said, "You can enter God's Kingdom only through the narrow gate. The highway to hell is broad, and its gate is wide for the many who choose that way. But the gateway to life is very narrow and the road is difficult, and only a few ever find it" (Matthew 7:13–14).

God's Word makes the path to life very clear, but human nature has difficulty accepting it. People are blinded by the folly

of this world, pursuing things that do not bring lasting fulfillment, joy, and peace.

Paul wrote to the church in Philippi:

> For I have told you often before, and I say it again with
> tears in my eyes, that there are many whose conduct
> shows they are really enemies of the cross of Christ.
> They are headed for destruction. Their god is their ap-
> petite, they brag about shameful things, and they think
> only about this life here on earth. (Philippians 3:18–19)

It's easy to "think only about this life here on earth." It's
what we see every day. But there is a spiritual realm, which is
far more important than the physical realm. We must be so in
tune with the Holy Spirit that we begin to see with spiritual
eyes. Only then can we discern between the temporal, un-
important things and the eternal things of God. This is the
path to life.

The Father of Lies, Satan, can even use good things to
distract us from the most important things. I used to place
my ministry above all else, and as a result, I was angry, out of
control, and miserable. People applauded and showered me

with praise. But I was not sensitive to the Spirit of God and was blinded to spiritual truth. It took a simple yet deeply spiritual man to see the truth of my situation. While others saw a powerful preacher, he saw a tormented man. And he helped me identify why I felt the way I did.

God is faithful, always waiting on us to yield to His will and purpose. When we get on our knees and submit our will to His, He restores us. We don't have to spend our lives "chasing cars." We can have fulfillment, peace, and joy when we surrender every impulse and desire to His direction and control. Paul wrote, "We are made right with God by placing our faith in Jesus Christ. And this is true for everyone who believes, no matter who we are" (Romans 3:22).

We are not dogs, enslaved to chasing our foolish desires to their final end. Jesus Christ offers us redemption, purpose, and life in Him. We just have to cease chasing other things and start chasing Him.

26

Set Your Eyes on the Prize

Animals possess an amazing ability to focus. A cat will stalk a bird for hours, creeping up a tree slowly and patiently. Our little Princess will chase a squirrel with complete disregard for anything else. Of course, she never catches one. They scamper up a tree too quickly, but once she sets her eyes on that prize, nothing else in the world exists.

The apostle Paul wrote, "Do you not know that in a race all the runners run, but only one gets the prize? Run in such a way as to get the prize" (1 Corinthians 9:24, NIV). His statement is not about becoming a better competitor, because there are no winners or losers in the Christian walk. His point is one of focus.

I have enjoyed watching the performances of amazing

athletes like US swimmer Michael Phelps, who was so impressive in the 2008 Olympics. He accumulated more gold medals than any other athlete and broke world records every time he hit the pool. Those who know him credit his success to his remarkable focus on his sport. Sure, he's naturally talented, but he also works hard to do one thing: win.

Betty enjoys watching figure skating. It's remarkable the way the men and women gracefully fly around the rink, despite the distraction of the lights, music, and crowd. For years these athletes endure rigorous training, mentally and physically, with a single goal in mind.

We've seen this type of focus in other athletes. Jack Nicklaus, Peyton Manning, Wayne Gretzky, and Josh Hamilton come to mind. They all illustrate the potential for individuals to excel beyond normal expectations and achieve greatness.

And often great athletes attribute much of their success to influential people in their lives. Michael Phelps was quoted by ESPN as saying, "I don't think I could be where I am today with any other coach. He's so intelligent in this sport and cares about every one of his athletes. He's so thorough. He's always on top of things. I'm fortunate to have a coach like him." Phelps was talking about Bob Bowman, the American swimming coach.

Another swim coach said, "Bob teaches him, advises him, guides him, pushes him."[7]

All of us can achieve remarkable things in life if we are focused. Granted, it will likely be on a smaller stage than the Olympics or the Masters, but we can truly be who we were created to be if we will set our goals, work to achieve them, and refuse to be distracted by the obstacles in our way.

We need the focus of the cat watching the bird in the tree.

To do this, it often takes someone to teach us and guide us. Yet coaches are not always there for our comfort. Like Bowman, they will push us and challenge us to be better. As Christians, we look to Jesus Christ as our "life coach." His words constantly push us and challenge us. By focusing on His principles, I have become far more than I could have been on my own. Any success I have had in life is directly attributed to His "coaching." He tells me (and you) things like this: "No one who puts his hand to the plow and looks back is fit for service in the kingdom of God" (Luke 9:62, NIV). Like an Olympic athlete, once we set our course to follow Christ, we don't turn back; we press forward with our eyes on the ultimate goal. We prepare mentally and spiritually to finish the race that is our life with nothing less than "gold" in mind.

Like the US athletes who wrap themselves in the American flag at the end of a race well run, we seek to wrap ourselves in the glory of Jesus Christ as the music of heaven celebrates our efforts. There could be no greater glory than to hear the Lord say to us, "Well done, my good and faithful servant!" (Matthew 25:21).

Following Christ is more like a marathon than a sprint, so we must set our eyes on Him every single day in every circumstance and "throw off everything that hinders and the sin that so easily entangles, and let us run with perseverance the race marked out for us" (Hebrews 12:1, NIV).

The beautiful thing about the Christian life is that even if we stumble, we are not out of the race, because we are not competing with other people. We are measured according to God's expectations for us while being carried by His grace. There is no silver or bronze, only gold. And the medal is waiting for each of us if we will just stay in the race. Like the apostle Paul, we must forget what is behind and strain toward what is ahead, pressing on toward the goal to win the prize for which God has called us heavenward in Christ Jesus (see Philippians 3:13–14, NIV).

I have had the honor of visiting with skater Scott Hamilton, who carried the American flag in the opening ceremony of the 1980 Winter Olympics in Lake Placid, New York, and won the gold medal in 1984. He knows what it's like to have a good coach. Scott says that spiritual coaching, as found in God's Word, guides us through all our challenges: relationship issues, job stress, financial difficulties, and everything else. "God is the Almighty Coach," Hamilton says. "He always has all the information right there in front of us at the right time. It's all there; we just need to open our eyes, minds, and hearts."[8]

The world will try to distract us, but the Lord is there to help us keep our focus. Like a dog chasing a squirrel and an athlete chasing the gold, we must purposefully and persistently pursue the higher calling Jesus has for us.

27

She Follows Me

Princess likes to follow me everywhere I go. If I sit down, she stares at me or jumps up onto my lap, either looking into my eyes or curling up in the cradle of my arm. Sometimes she obviously wants to play with one of her squeaky toys or plead for a treat. Other times it is as if she is wondering what I am thinking or doing. She seems to ask, "Where are you going?" Whatever my plans, she does not want to miss out.

One day as I pondered her actions, I wondered if God notices our interest in what He is doing or what He desires to do and if He's pleased that we are keeping a close eye on Him. I often realize I am not giving much attention to what He is doing. I am too much in my own world to consider His movements and actions. Surely God notices when we are waiting on

Him, looking to Him, and interested in what He desires to do and know what is on His heart.

I find more joy, peace, and fulfillment when I focus on God, rather than myself, and truly seek with all my heart to follow Him. Jesus said, "Follow Me, and I will make you fishers of men" (Matthew 4:19, NASB). In other words, when we are actually following Him, we will notice others and reach out to them with love and concern. We will be a part of the net bringing in the harvest for His glory. In more than fifty years of personal and public ministry, I have seen the results of God-given concern for others. There is no end to the positive effect that broken hearts and true tears of concern can have. It really is the promise of God that they who go forth sowing and weeping will return bearing the good fruit of those tears and concern.

If I am looking at God, really watching Him and focusing on Him, I will rightly focus beyond my world and make a difference in someone else's. If we follow Him, we will lose our lives in His purpose and actually find real meaning for ourselves and our family. When we follow Him, we take up our cross daily, dying to fleshly and selfish desires. This is not a painful process if we are looking unto Jesus as "the author and finisher of our faith" (Hebrews 12:2, KJV).

It is truly amazing what happens inside our hearts when we are vitally interested in Him and His will. We can't take our eyes off Jesus, because He is the greatest attraction on the planet! When He moves, we move. When He rests, we rest. If He's excited, we're excited. If He weeps, we weep. We become His eyes, His hands, and truly an expression of His heart. As we move together, we reveal His body in all its fullness and glory.

28

So Hard to Say Good-Bye

The movie *Marley and Me* tells the story of the impact a dog had on a suburban family. Early in the movie, I commented to Betty, "Marley is the most out-of-control, destructive so-called pet I've ever seen. I don't think we could keep such an animal regardless of how cute he is."

Not too far into the story, however, we both fell in love with that golden mutt. At the end of the movie, tissues were not adequate. I had to get one of those blue shop towels. Dear God, how Betty and I cried!

I remember *Old Yeller* and not only how moved we were back then but also how it affected our children and grandchildren. It is so sad to say good-bye to a pet you love deeply.

As I write, our Princess is now eleven years old—eighty-four dog years. She has suddenly passed both Betty and me in age, even though it seems like yesterday when she was just a puppy. She has noticeably slowed down. She is not as quick, she does not race around as often, and her zeal to hunt (simply chasing squirrels and rabbits) has lessened. She's still okay—just different (kind of like me). The fire is still inside, but zealous expression and all-out activity have slowed drastically. Betty and I wonder if our kids and grandkids notice that about us. We do see it in Princess, and the exciting moments and outbursts of energy are more precious every day.

I think of her beautiful black fur coat, her expressive brown eyes with such a piercing stare, the fastest tongue on the planet, and her warm snuggle in my arm each morning and evening. I can't bear the thought of her not being here.

As might be expected, dachshunds are subject to spinal problems. If my spine were proportionately that long, I would be nine feet tall! Also, dachshunds are subject to arthritis. Princess can't jump as high anymore. We frequently have to help her up onto the sofa and into the pickup truck.

A few days ago I was sitting in the backyard watching her sniff every bush, tree trunk, and suspicious rock. Through the years I have often watched Princess with a big smile on my face and on some occasions with concern for her safety. However, I let her approach potential problem areas as I softly say, "Be careful." If danger seems imminent, I say firmly, "Princess, stop!"

God uses a similar tactic with me. I have heard God's still, small voice of cautious concern. It seems our Father seldom shouts, but the consequences of bad choices certainly do. I wonder why God doesn't shout more often. Perhaps He does but we don't want to hear.

As I've already mentioned, we once had a beautiful long-hair, red-coated dachshund named Heidi. She looked like a tiny, short-legged Irish setter. As she approached her fifteenth year, she became very hard of hearing, and her vision dimmed. It was sad. So it is too often with Christians, but not because of old age. Because of indifference.

When Heidi was run over by the car, no doubt her hearing loss and dim vision played a role. Our family wept, and we had a special burial service for her. We built a small rock monument for her in the backyard. I don't like to think about it even as I write.

Recently my youngest daughter told me about reaching a point where they had to put their dog down because of health-related issues. I hate the idea of that! Betty and I have asked ourselves, could we do that with Princess? How would we deal with it? Seems strange, doesn't it, as we are talking about "just a pet." But that's the thing; they are not just pets. They are family! It is amazing how true this is.

As our grandchildren have become teenagers and young adults—not so needful anymore of time with Mimi and Papaw—our dachshund has received even more of our attention and affection. The word *close* doesn't begin to explain the reality. I don't ever want to see Princess suffer because of painful difficulties resulting from her age, and I continually pray that serious disease is never a factor. Whether by tragic accident, as with Heidi, or some other cause, our future heartache is difficult to contemplate.

Betty has said that she can't bear the thought. My eyes are filling with tears as I consider this very real possibility. We both want to be with her at the vet's if she must be put to sleep. To be honest, as I consider that dreaded moment, I think I would want her in my arms when she leaves so she will know she is so very, very close to my heart. I want her little face next to mine and my cheek against those long, silky black ears. I am convinced weeping will last more than a day, but as God promises, joy will come in the morning,[9] and I will be remembering the best of times we shared with Princess—truly precious memories—and they will last as long as I live.

Betty has said she wants to be close to Princess too when

she goes, telling her how pretty she is, how much we love her, and what a joy she has always been. The expressions we will share exemplify how we should feel and do feel, not just about a dear, loyal pet, but about our loved ones. Perhaps anticipating or remembering the loss of a simple pet can serve as a reminder to share with others how special they are and how meaningful it is to know them.

When we say good-bye to Princess, even in our brokenness our hearts will overflow with gratitude for the fact that she was a part of giving more meaning and joy to us.

Will we see our pets in heaven? My answer is, "If you want them to be there, then yes!" Can I prove it? No. But I don't have to because God knows best and always wants the very best for His children.

Randy Alcorn talks about this in his book *Heaven:*

> Our beloved dog recently died. Should I correct my kids when they say they can't wait to play with Rocky again in Heaven? Humorist Will Rogers said, "If there are no dogs in heaven, then when I die I want to go where they went." This statement was, of course, based on sentiment, not theology. However, it reflects something biblical: a God-given affection for animals.[10]

That's why the question of whether pets will be in heaven is not as stupid as some assume. In his book *In Light of Eternity,* Alcorn says: "Animals aren't nearly as valuable as people and they don't have eternal souls, but God is their maker and has touched many people's lives through them. It would be simple for him to recreate a pet in heaven if this would bring his children joy."[11] He's the giver of all good gifts, not the taker of them. If it would please us to have a pet restored to the new earth, that may be sufficient reason.

We do know that animals will be on the new earth, which is a redeemed and restored old earth on which animals had a prominent role. Romans 8:21–23 assumes animals as part of a suffering creation eagerly awaiting deliverance through humanity's resurrection. This seems to require that some animals that lived, suffered, and died on the old earth must be made whole on the new earth. Wouldn't a number of those likely be our pets?

In her excellent book *Holiness in Hidden Places,* Joni Eareckson Tada says:

> If God brings our pets back to life, it wouldn't surprise me. It would be just like Him. It would be totally in keeping with His generous character…. Exorbitant.

Excessive. Extravagant in grace after grace. Of all the
dazzling discoveries and ecstatic pleasures heaven will
hold for us, the potential of seeing Scrappy would be
pure whimsy—utterly, joyfully, surprisingly super-
fluous.... Heaven is going to be a place that will refract
and reflect in as many ways as possible the goodness
and joy of our great God, who delights in lavishing love
on His children.[12]

In a poem about the world to come, theologian John Piper
wrote:

> And as I knelt beside the brook
> To drink eternal life, I took
> A glance across the golden grass,
> And saw my dog, old Blackie, fast
> As she could come. She leaped the stream—
> Almost—and what a happy gleam
> Was in her eye. I knelt to drink.
> And knew that I was on the brink
> Of endless joy. And everywhere
> I turned I saw a wonder there.[13]

We needn't be embarrassed to grieve the loss of our pets or to want to see them again. If we believe that God is their creator, that He loves us and them, and that He intends to restore His creatures from the bondage they experienced because of our sin, then we have biblical grounds for not only wanting but expecting that we may be with them again on the new earth.

So let's not correct our kids when they pray they'll be able to see their pets again. The answer to that prayer is up to God. He loves to hear the prayers of His children, and there is scriptural reason to believe He may answer those prayers. Remember that our children's instinctive grasp of heaven—and what we should look forward to there—is sometimes better than ours.

For me, I expect to see in heaven any pet that holds a special place in my heart. Joy will be no less, however, if I am mistaken. The glory that fills all of heaven will fill every area of my life, and there will be no void. I will praise God for every blessing and precious memory for all of eternity, and pets like Princess will be among those precious thoughts.

Thank You, Father, for all You have taught me through my pets…and all the other wonderful creatures of Your creation.

Notes

1. "To Help Deer—Don't Feed Them: Feeding Can Do More Harm Than Good," Colorado Department of Natural Resources, Colorado Division of Wildlife, http://wildlife.state.co.us/WildlifeSpecies /LivingWithWildlife/Mammals/Pages/HelpDeer.aspx.
2. "Pet Statistics," ASPCA, www.aspca.org/about-us/faq /pet-statistics.aspx.
3. Associated Press, "Birds Didn't Have Flu, They Were Drunk," CBSNews.com, April 27, 2009, www.cbsnews .com/stories/2006/02/02/world/main1273456.shtml.
4. Science Digest, "Birds May Have Been Dead Drunk," *Seattle Times,* February 5, 2008, http://seattletimes .nwsource.com/html/nationworld/2004164318 _sciencedig05.html.
5. "Drunk Birds Give Airport Trouble," Birding.UK.com, July 25, 2006, www.birding.uk.com/bird-news/15 -international-bird-news/98-drunk-birds-give-airport -trouble.

6. Associated Press, "Birds Didn't Have Flu."

7. Pat Forde, "Intense? Insane? Maybe, but Bowman Is *the* Architect of Phelps' Quest," ESPN, http://sports.espn .go.com/oly/summer08/columns/story?columnist =forde_pat&id=3534490.

8. Scott Hamilton, *The Great Eight: How to Be Happy (Even When You Have Every Reason to Be Miserable)* (Nashville: Thomas Nelson, 2009), 36.

9. See Psalm 30:5.

10. Randy Alcorn, *Heaven* (Wheaton: Tyndale, 2004), 385.

11. Randy Alcorn, *In Light of Eternity: Perspectives on Heaven* (Colorado Springs, CO: WaterBrook, 1999), 30.

12. Joni Eareckson Tada, *Holiness in Hidden Places* (Nashville: Thomas Nelson, 1999), 135.

13. John Piper, *Future Grace* (Sisters, OR: Multnomah, 1995), 381. Used by permission.

About the Authors

JAMES ROBISON is the founder and president of LIFE Outreach International, a worldwide Christian relief organization. He is also the host of *LIFE Today,* a daily syndicated television program that reaches three hundred million homes in the United States, Canada, Europe, and Australia. He is the author of many books, including *Indivisible, The Absolutes, True Prosperity,* and *Living in Love,* and has spoken to millions of people through evangelistic crusades since entering public ministry in 1962.

JAMES RANDALL ROBISON is the son of James and Betty Robison. He works as a writer, producer, and host for *LIFE Today.* He is also the author of *God Wants You to Be Happy.*

*"**James and Betty must know something.** Spend any moments near them, and you quickly detect, and enjoy, an uncommon affection. I pray that we learn from their experience."*

—MAX LUCADO, pastor and best-selling author

James and Betty Robison, co-hosts of the syndicated TV show *LIFE Today*, share secrets from their almost 50 years of marriage. Let the Robisons show you how to be more in love now than you were as a newlywed.

Read an excerpt at www.waterbrookmultnomah.com!

Printed in the United States
by Baker & Taylor Publisher Services